Home Alterations and Repairs

 THE COMPLETE HANDBOOK

PAUL HYMERS

NEW HOLLAND

DEDICATION

For Karina

First published in 2004 by New Holland Publishers (UK) Ltd
Garfield House, 86–88 Edgware Road
London W2 2EA
United Kingdom
London • Cape Town • Sydney • Auckland
www.newhollandpublishers.com

ISBN 1 84330 695 6

Senior Editor: Clare Sayer
Editor: Ian Kearey
Designer: Casebourne Rose Design Associates
Illustrator: Sue Rose
Cover photograph: AG&G Books

Printed and bound by Kyodo Printing Co (Singapore) Pte Ltd

DECLARATION

The views expressed in this book are those of the author and do not necessarily reflect those of his
employers.

The publishers have made every effort to ensure that the information contained in this book is
correct at the time of going to press. All recommendations are made without guarantee on the part
of the author and the publishers. The author and publishers disclaim any liability for damages or
injury resulting from use of this information.

Contents

Introduction

Rumour has it that there are some countries in the developed world where people buy homes and never alter or change them at all. They never add windows, never knock through walls, never re-cover the roof or re-model the bathroom. Never change anything. Weird, isn't it? In the UK we can't leave our homes alone – there is always something that needs changing and improving, and rightly so.

Homes can always be improved, even brand-new ones – especially brand-new ones – because we all live our own lifestyle to the needs of ourselves and our families. Of course you can always make do with your home the way it is, or sell up and move, but adapting it to suit you can be surprisingly easy, once you recognise what is possible.

To remove an internal wall and open two rooms into one will change at a stroke the way you use your home. Moving the staircase can open up all kinds of possibilities – and simply adding a window can brighten your life.

The light of day is a much undervalued thing, at least it has been since Window Tax was abolished in 1822. We humans hate darkness. Light elevates the soul – it makes us feel good to walk into a room that is flooded by daylight. And if sunlight beams in at certain times, it adds joy and warmth to that feeling. Installing a window that lets the morning sunshine in while you eat breakfast is priceless.

Creating a wall of glass from floor to ceiling extends a room into a garden. Indeed, with the right colour, décor and frameless glazing, the room can appear to be part of the garden, taking you outside the house in your armchair.

If we are to get the best from our homes, they will need to be repaired from time to time; and if properly done, repairs should be considered as improvements too. A property that has been properly maintained is a strengthened property and one that should outlast and outsell its neighbours on the same street.

This, the third complete handbook in the series, aims at opening up the possibilities for alterations and repairs, both structural and non-structural, and at guiding you through them towards a better home.

CHAPTER 1

Preliminaries

Given half a chance, any building will give the impression that it has been formed from a tablet of stone and can't be changed. It's an illusion; buildings can be altered and should be altered to suit the needs of those who occupy them. With homes, those needs change as people grow, families expand and shrink, and new owners move in. To expect the place to be the perfect home throughout all of that, without any modification, is a little unreasonable and unnecessary.

Minor alterations can change your home for the better in a matter of days. Taking down a wall between the kitchen and the dining room will let you talk to your family and guests while you cook. Putting up a partition to separate a living room from a dining room will create another reception room and an extra space in which to relax or socialise separately. With the whole family wanting to use the bathroom in the same mad hour of the day, creating an en-suite in your master bedroom will relieve the stress.

If you think a different layout for your home would suit your present lifestyle but would be too difficult to achieve, think again. Homes are not irreversibly built, and most will see many changes in their lifetime; changes that are easily accomplished, given imagination and will.

Home ownership is often described as 'a very psychological phenomenon'. The ownership of our home means more to us than just its monetary value. It's our cave, our own little space in an increasingly crowded world. Even so, in the UK we are particularly obsessed with the value of our homes. Soon it will take over from the weather as our most talked-about subject. Values have gone up by a staggering amount in the last 50 years – so much so that if they rise at the same rate in the next 50, the average house price in 2073 will be £5,000,000!

So it follows that we do want to improve them, but we also want to see those improvements add value to the property that we own.

Which alteration?

Most alteration projects will add value if carried out properly and with care, but some are more profitable than others. Those alterations that are particularly profitable include:

● Creating off-street parking

● Installing a shower (particularly an en-suite shower room)

● Adding windows and bringing in light

● Fitting out the kitchen

● Fitting out the bathroom

● Restoring or exposing original (period) features, like beams and fireplaces

A few non-starter projects that can remove value from your home are:

● Artificial stone cladding

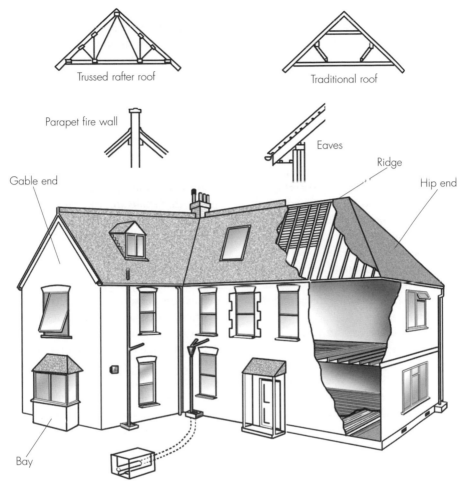

Trussed rafter roof

Traditional roof

Parapet fire wall

Eaves

Ridge

Gable end

Hip end

Bay

A survey will identify the constructional elements of your home.

- Fitting secondary glazing that doesn't open

- Removing or covering original (period) features

- Creating inner bedrooms that can only be accessed from another room

- Creating windowless rooms with no natural light

Surveying your home
Initial survey

With most home-improvement projects, the more you know about your home the easier it is to alter and repair it. Start by collecting information with a survey on a room-by-room basis, and build up a picture of where the walls on each floor align and where they don't.

Measuring your rooms and plotting them to scale on a simple line drawing

7

will tell you a lot. To start with, this should reveal how thick your internal walls are, and which of them are continued upstairs. Continuous walls are normally load-bearing walls, and are likely to support the floor structure and possibly the roof as well. With older homes, traditional floorboards reveal which way the floor joists run (at right angles to the lengths of board), but in modern homes chipboard sheeting is harder to read and it's often necessary to lift a piece up. Remember that the floor joists in one room can run in the opposing direction to the joists in another, so don't assume they all run the same way. Architects will look for the shortest spans when designing the floors in homes.

It makes sense to start your measuring in the rooms upstairs and work your way down. Ideally use graph tracing paper, so that you can keep it all square and overlay the floor layouts to see where walls and services align. Partitions in upstairs rooms that aren't continued from walls below are either supported by the floor joists themselves or by a beam. Beam downstands are visible, of course, even though they may be boxed in, but sometimes beams are installed within the depth of the floor structure, and you will only be able to see them by lifting the floorboarding.

I really do believe that you have to live in your home for quite a while before you know whether it works for you, or how you could improve on it. I guess some of us know straight away what alterations we want to make when moving into a new place, but it's amazing how things change once

you've lived there for a while – for instance, ideas on how the rooms could be better linked by a repositioned door, or how a new window on the stairs could really brighten it up and reduce your electricity bill.

When your wall layouts are complete, add the positions of doors and windows and then the services and bathroom and kitchen fittings. In some homes, the water supply and waste pipes are visible and can easily be plotted, but in others they may be built into the structure and hidden.

Finding the services

Finding out where your services arrive and where they run through your home is often tricky, and is sometimes not possible without electronic detectors. All the service companies now use these detectors to plot their services in your garden, and you should contact them in advance to determine their position if you have excavations to do outside. Gas, electric, water and phone can all arrive below ground to your home, and drainage or underpinning excavation work can reveal them unexpectedly. You can buy similar but cheaper detectors from DIY stores for tracing services inside the floors and walls of your home.

With drainage, you can lift manhole covers and run water from various appliances to see where the connections for each are made and which way the drains run. It is easy to check drains for alignment and continuity by placing a torch at one manhole and holding an angled mirror in the next. A straight pipe that is not deformed or bent will reveal the torch lamp. Not all drains, however, are that obliging. In some properties the drainage is a mystery, to say the least. A number of manholes may exist in the garden (some buried), servicing separate foul and surface water systems. You may even have the added attraction of redundant drains or shared drainage passing over your property from a neighbouring building.

Private drainage has no official records, unlike public sewers, which have to be surveyed and mapped, so it can often prove difficult to trace. Start by looking for plans at the local authority offices or Land Registry. If you know that drainage alterations have been carried out in recent years, it 'might' be possible to trace the Building Regulations application and view the plans as the owner of the property. I say might because Building Control records are not required to be accessible to the public in the same way as Planning Application records. Otherwise, and unless you happen to be a whizz with the divining rods, it is the trial-and-error method of running water and looking down manholes.

Detailed survey

A more specific or detailed survey may have to be carried out for some projects, and this is likely to mean engaging a professional, perhaps as part of the design work. Structural engineers can work from detailed plans, but if there are any errors or omissions on them, it follows that these will be replicated in the structural design. Most structural engineers will want to inspect your home themselves if they are designing structural alterations for it, and this should certainly be encouraged, even if you have detailed plans for the property.

There is a world of difference between structural designing for alterations and for new buildings or extensions. For the latter, engineers can safely work from plans of yet-to-be-built construction. With alteration work, the construction already exists and needs to be investigated and recorded accurately. Only in this way will an engineer or designer be able to safely specify the work. Your previous survey will be invaluable, but professionals will need to check and measure up the areas of load being applied to new beams and walls for themselves. Outside your home where the tape measure can't reach, the height of walls and chimneys can be calculated by counting the brick courses and mortar beds.

The species and strength of existing timber isn't always easy to identify, but if need be a small sample can be taken and sent to the Building Research Establishment (BRE) or the Timber Research and Development Association (TRADA) for identification.

Home logbooks

When you buy a new or used car you expect to receive a logbook with it and a specification, plus a record of its service history – so is it unreasonable to expect the same when you spend a hundred times as much on a home?

Historically, all we've had for our money in terms of information is the deeds (and extraordinarily, we don't

SECTION 1: STRUCTURE	
Walls	Type and insulation
Floors	Type and insulation
Roofs	Type and insulation

SECTION 2: SERVICES	
Space heating	Boiler and system details, controls and instructions
Hot water	Storage system details, controls and instructions
Water supply	Supply authority, position of stopcock and service entry point.
	Details of any fitted softeners or limescale reducers.
Electricity	Circuit layouts, distribution board type, RCD positions,
	MCB/fuse labelling
Gas	Position of gas points and incoming supply
Phone	Position of phone entry and ducting, service type

SECTION 3: WINDOWS AND DOORS
Type, glazing, security system – locks, alarms, etc., position of emergency escape windows

SECTION 4: DRAINAGE	
Foul water	Sewer mains/cesspool/septic tank. Plans
Surface water	Sewer mains/soakaway. Plans

SECTION 5: PLANS, APPROVALS, ETC.
Copies of Planning Permissions, Building Regulation Approvals and other legal consents and agreements

SECTION 6: MAINTENANCE SCHEDULE
A schedule of regular maintenance and servicing needs, with dates of attendance
(see examples in Chapter 7)

cven get to keep those – if we have a mortgage the lender thoughtfully hangs on to them for us, and once we've closed the mortgage sells them back to us), and, as most of us have found out, the deeds won't tell you where the drainage runs or where the water supply stopcock is. Useful information about your home is hard to find.

Commercial building owners keep a logbook containing the details of the building's construction and services and so on – information that is valuable for routine maintenance and repairs, not just when the building changes occupants. A home logbook would serve to do the same, and could become an official document when homes are bought and sold.

Plans have already been developed to introduce a system of compulsory Home Reports carried out by registered Home Inspectors, to provide reputable and reliable information about properties. Estate agents are not pleased about this, as it rather takes away the glamour and mystery of selling properties on the strength of location and a nice kitchen. They've always been able to take the focus away from a collapsing roof, or an unauthorised loft conversion, by pointing out how nicely appointed the bathroom is. The new system looks at the nuts and bolts of homes, and draws attention to some of the surprises new home-owners have in store for them in the future.

Keeping a home logbook will provide more information about your home than a Home Report will show, and offering more information about your home will enhance its prospects of sale. Yes, yes – you will still be able to paint all the walls cream, bring in a corkscrew willow plant and brew fresh coffee before a showing, but also you will be able to tell buyers how the central heating works. It'll be a new approach – honesty in home-selling – but in time, and with a new breed of estate agents, it could catch on.

Over a period of time you could gradually build up your own home logbook with information. It would be divided into sections, similar to a Home Report, as shown opposite.

Each of these sections can be enhanced with information as and when required, thus building up a picture of information on your home. When it's complete, the next time an electrician calls to wire in some new sockets, you'll be able to show how the circuits are divided up, saving you time and money.

Preparing for contractors

Where schemes of alteration and repair are based on letters of agreement or detailed contracts, conditions that aim to minimise the disruption caused by the work can be included. This includes the hours of starting and finishing work for both weekdays and weekends, the protection of your home and garden, etc., but it isn't reasonable, or indeed practical, to prescribe everything, and some disruption to everyday living is inevitable. For the most part it is enough to establish with the contractor a bond of mutual respect, where work can proceed efficiently and you can continue to live in the property. Even so, it is worth discussing the arrangements for some particular areas where conflict can, and often does arise, before work starts.

Waste disposal

The removal of waste and debris from the site as work proceeds is a popular bone of contention. Some contractors just let it build up until the job is done. Rubbish and debris should be removed at the end of each day. Carpenters and bricklayers are often the worst offenders, discarding offcuts of wood and broken bricks, mortar and insulation leftovers. It needs to be regularly collected in an agreed place (preferably outside) or taken to the skip, where it can be removed from the site altogether. It's not unreasonable to expect each trade to be accompanied by a labourer who, as well as serving the materials to work with, also removes the waste and keeps the work area clean.

Safety

Keeping any site tidy will go a long way to keeping it safe, and where space is tight, the contractor will help himself as well as you by keeping it so. Foundation trenches and open holes should be covered with strong boards or fenced off, and at least one entrance to the home should be retained with a clear access. As the home-owner, it is your responsibility to ensure the safety of visitors to your home, so don't leave it down to the builder's discretion to decide what is OK – check for yourself.

Facilities

Agree on what facilities will be available to the workers, at least verbally if not by written condition. If you're going to be at home for the most part if not all of the project, then the use of the bathroom for sanitary purposes would be reasonable. If you aren't, then the workers may need to hire a portaloo.

It is seldom thought of as a good idea to let painters, decorators and plasterers have the use of the bathroom for cleaning themselves or their tools at the end of the day. These trades are messy and worthy of being washed down outside. Bath and basin waste pipes can become blocked easily when brushes, rollers and trowels are cleaned indoors.

Most contractors have their own cellphones now, and shouldn't need to rely on your phone to communicate, but you may be happy for them to receive incoming calls while they are here, if it helps them to organise their work on your home.

Electricity isn't such a sticking point – with the use of petrol generators for heavy-duty tools, and with powerful cordless hand tools, most jobs can be done without overusing the domestic electricity supply.

A lot of water goes into home improvements, and it has to come from somewhere. An outside tap is ideal, but if that isn't possible, the contractor can always fill water butts at the beginning of each day from a hose connection and use the stored water. In any event you will want cement mortar, concrete and plaster to be mixed outside.

Protecting your home
Dust covers
You can never have enough dustsheets down when building work is underway,

particularly when it comes to taking down internal walls or chimneys.

These jobs can be done with care and a limited amount of mess, but this way takes time and involves small hand tools. If you haven't specified that you want the job done considerately with hammer and bolster rather than sledgehammer or electric disc-cutter, then you can expect to be finding dust for weeks to come. It pays to discuss how it will be done and when it will be done before the work starts, and use plenty of dust sheets and good ventilation when it does.

You can expect some tradesmen to cover a few things with dustsheets, but if you want to protect your own home, you should expect to have to do it yourself. By its nature, dust always arrives in greater volume than you predict and always spreads to parts you thought it would never reach. You can't do enough to limit its fall, but you can reduce the amount of hoovering and dusting you have to do afterwards.

The repair work of re-covering your roof with new tiles can generate a phenomenal amount of black dust when old slates are removed. Your attic will be covered in it, as will the insulation and anything else you leave up there. Pack everything up in sealed boxes, or better still, remove it beforehand and roll up the insulation out of the way. Dustsheets should be spread out over the ceiling, and the loft hatch needs to remain shut for the duration. Once the builders have some of the old covering off, they will be able to gain access from the scaffold and won't need to use the loft hatch.

You can use polythene sheeting to cover furniture, but it isn't ideal for floors since it easily gets rucked up and is slippery to walk on – old cotton sheets are far better.

Painters working on the outside often prefer to use ladders to scaffold towers, but there is still every reason to insist they use a heavy dustsheet beneath them as they work along. Not only will it keep your pathways and garden free of any spilt new paint, it should also catch the dust and debris from removing old paint. Scaffold towers do make protection easier in this respect, but make sure the ladders are removed from them at the end of each day to keep your home safe from chance intruders.

Stair tread covers

Wooden stairs need to be protected while work is ongoing, and the only proper way to do this is to cover the treads with cardboard taped into position. If you've experienced the challenge of trying to get down a staircase covered in washing, you'll know it isn't safe to use any form of dustsheet on a stair.

Carpet protection

Carpet fitters on building sites have long had the problem of trying to finish their work before it's ruined with dirty footprints. To overcome this they use rolled brown paper, like backing paper, and if you have floor finishings you'd really like to protect, make sure this appears in your home. It doesn't have to cover every inch of the floor, so long as a wide enough walkway is marked out across rooms and the joints are overlapped and taped down.

Covering smoke alarms

Smoke detectors are sensitive to dust, and to avoid them being repeatedly triggered or damaged by clouds of dust during demolition or building work, they should be covered over. The makers of alarms provide plastic covers that fit snugly over them for this purpose; it doesn't matter if you no longer have the covers, a plastic bag and an elastic band will do the same job, and so, it seems, will rubber gloves (at least I think what I saw was a rubber glove). The important thing to remember is that at the end of every working day, when the dust has settled, the covers should be removed and the alarms left active at night. Do not be tempted to disconnect them for the duration of the project, they are there to protect you – as the owners of Windsor Castle will tell you, the chance of an accidental fire starting is higher when you're having work done on the place.

Listed buildings and VAT

The owners of listed buildings have enjoyed VAT- free alterations and repairs on their homes for a long time, and this shows every sign of continuing. Only the Customs and Excise office will be able to confirm that it has, of course, because, like anything to do with tax, things can change with every budget event. This VAT exemption is valid for works which require Listed Building Consent, and not for those that don't.

Scaffolding

Lightweight scaffold towers are ideal for decorating work. Made up of H sections and cross-braces, they can be assembled, dismantled and relocated fairly quickly. If you're redecorating fascias and soffits or replacing gutters, they offer you a safe working platform that lets you work alongside the eaves, rather than beneath them on a ladder. You can hire scaffold towers from most plant hire companies, and all you need to do is recognise that they do have limitations: they have a maximum height, which should never be extended, and at all costs you should avoid the temptation to lean from them. I have known people topple them over after abusing both of these issues, with near-fatal consequences.

For a professional scaffold, some basic safety checks should be done each day by you, the owner, and whoever is working on it:

● Check that it is firmly seated on baseplates that haven't sunk into the ground when the roof tiles are taken up or after it has rained

● Check that the kickboards at the edges of the platform haven't been left off

● Check that the handrail pole hasn't been removed to bring materials up and left off afterwards

● Check that the boards are all there and no gaps or unsupported boards (traps) are present

- Check that the top of any ladder is tied to the scaffold

You should be able to do all of these checks from the ground looking up; if not, engage your contractors to do them for you.

Scaffolds that are erected on your property boundary or against a public highway are a particular risk and may need to be enclosed with catchment nets or brick guards to prevent falling material. It is advisable to specify that you want the scaffold erected in accordance with BS:5973, particularly if you are employing the scaffolder directly, rather than your contractor.

Neighbours

Keeping your neighbours informed about the work may not be a high priority, but it is extraordinary how many complaints are received by local councils from aggrieved neighbours over building works. Complaints range from the parking of contractors' vehicles in the road outside, to noise and loss of privacy from scaffold-borne workmen. You may not be able to do anything about some of their objections, but in specific areas they do have rights.

The Party Wall, Etc. Act 1996 requires you to notify neighbours two months in advance of any work proposed to a party wall with their property. A process of consultation must be followed to include their considerations. The Act not only covers work to shared indoor walls but also shared garden walls and even excavations near to the boundary – in some situations, 'near' may be as distant as 6 m. The Act does not apply to drilling into walls for minor fixings, for shelving, etc., chasing out for power points and light fittings, or indeed re-plastering. It does include work such as bearing a beam onto a party wall, inserting a DPC or repairing the wall, which you have the right to do, but still must follow the procedures laid down.

Advice on the Party Wall, Etc. Act 1996 should be sought, and a surveyor should be appointed if necessary. Party wall surveyors can be found on the registers of professional associations such as the RICS (Royal Institution of Chartered Surveyors), ABE (Association of Building Engineers) and ASI (Architecture and Surveying Institute), In addition there is the Pyramus & Thisbe Club (which is a society of specialist party wall surveyors, and is not a Shakespearean amateur dramatics group).

Flats and maisonettes

These are different to single-family homes because they have a common entrance and escape. The design or nature of any improvements can be affected when you have this situation, as flats and maisonettes have special requirements for fire safety that don't apply to single-family homes. Because of these common parts to the building and the need for them to be kept safe and free from fire and smoke, alterations to the layout of your own flat are limited.

Ongoing controls exist under the form of the Housing Act, in which they are described as 'Homes In Multiple Occupation' (HMOs) – an unfortunate acronym that somehow makes them sound as though they're connected with the prison service. Any building divided up into flats can be covered by this legislation and regularly inspected to ensure it is up to standard. Improvement notices can be served on the landlords to improve it if it doesn't come up to scratch.

The entrance doors of individual flats should normally be at least half-hour fire doors, self-closing with intumescent seals around the edges. Internal doors, behind the flat lobby, should be 20-minute fire doors, and the flat itself should be laid out to ensure you don't have far to travel to get to the door. The position of the kitchen is of primary importance: you should not have to pass through it to get out from the sleeping and living areas. Kitchens shouldn't be relocated to create this situation.

Rented and ex-rented homes

Alterations and some repairs to privately rented homes will usually need the consent of the landlord or controlling management company, and this would be the place to start with any proposals you have. There is little point in preparing detailed plans and applying for Planning Permission or Building Regulation approval if your landlord will not allow the work to be done at all.

Likewise, if you rent your home from the local authority or a housing association, you will need to obtain their general consent for any proposed work. Doubtless they will have the responsibility to repair and maintain the property, but for alteration work you will need their approval beyond that of Planning or Building Regulations.

There may be clauses in your tenancy agreement that require you to leave the property as you found it, and while these wouldn't prevent you from doing alterations, the landlords might want you to undo them should your tenancy end. In the case of removing or putting up non-loadbearing walls, that needn't be much of a problem, but creating structural alterations on a 'temporary basis' could be expensive, and so it is best to obtain confirmation from landlords of the status of any consent they give.

In the case of ex-council homes, local authorities normally impose conditions on the sale that require owners to still obtain their consent for a few years after the sale. Again, this is separate to anything else. It's often the case that homes are sold off sporadically in a street, leaving council-owned property dotted among private. I think this situation may trouble council landlords if alterations to the private ones affect their neighbouring properties, and so long as this doesn't appear likely, they should give their consent for the work to be done. You should always start by contacting your local authority's Housing Department and seeking their written consent before proceeding.

CHAPTER 2

Planning and Design

Appointing a professional designer

For some projects of alteration and repair a 'design' may not be needed at all: a specification will be enough. The difference is a subtle one, since specifications are in effect written designs, but it will help you decide whether or not you should appoint a professional to guide you.

Inviting builders around to quote on strengthening a roof or replacing a beam without any plan or written specification is a bit hit-and-miss, to say the least. If you invite six builders around, you are likely to find that five builders turn up. All five will express a great interest in doing the work and promise to deliver quotations in the next week or two, but you will never here from two of them again, and the remaining three will provide wildly different estimates – eventually.

It isn't really their fault. They are being asked to do something but they don't know exactly what, which means they have to write the specification into their quotations (which will undoubtedly be 'estimates' and not 'quotes'). This can work fine, but if the job is at all complex or has unknown factors to it, it won't.

A design drawn out on a plan or a written specification is something you can both hang your hat on and measure any variations from as they occur. Structural alterations need to be approved under the Building Regulations, and consequently a design is usually necessary. Structural engineers are the professionals in this domain, and most architectural designers are not qualified, nor will they attempt, to specify structural design work. They will, however, sub-contract out this element of a project to an engineer. If all your project consists of is a structural alteration, then there is little benefit in employing an architectural designer at all. Cut out the middle man and go straight to an engineer: those with the Institute of Structural Engineers are fully qualified in domestic alteration work.

With underpinning projects that arise from subsidence claims, insurance companies often have a list of structural engineers they will use, and approved contractors to carry out the work. Do not be tempted to find your own without their approval.

Structural engineers prepare plans as well as calculations, so you can expect to receive a sketch plan, if not a full-size drawing, to accompany their work. This is important, because builders can't read calculations – drawings yes, and specifications mostly, but calculations never. There is little point in paying for a design that is unintelligible for those charged with following it, so look for clarity and detail above all else in the plans you receive.

When it comes to designing alteration work, you may have a clear idea of what you want to achieve, whether it be a new bathroom or an open-plan living room, and good design can mean finding a professional who can simply put the details to your ideas.

If you know how you want to use your home and how spaces relate to each other, but are not sure how best to achieve it, you might want to employ an interior designer – but pay some consideration to their technical abilities if you do have to alter the layout of your home to achieve this.

Most designers will offer a free consultation period to meet you in your home and discuss your ideas for the place. When making this appointment, you should invite them to bring along details of other homes they've worked on, and some references of past clients.

Professional fees

The professional associations that designers such as architects, surveyors and structural engineers subscribe to, tend not to publish guidance on the fees their members should charge. The only method of validating a professional's charges is to compare them with other similarly qualified individuals or practices. The associations do, however, provide standard forms of engagement that set out the conditions of the appointment and the scope of the service the professionals are providing you with, together with a brief of the project. The charges should be set out in this agreement, whether in the form of an hourly rate, a percentage of the contract sum, or a fixed fee. If you appoint a practice, it is reasonable expect the partners to be fully qualified, but their assistants are likely not to be.

It might seem ironic that the designers and surveyors in the building industry are collectively referred to as 'professionals'. Practices are likely to employ young 'professionals' in training to keep their costs down, and you can expect to pay a reduced hourly rate for those engaged in your project. A firm of chartered surveyors, for example, may only consist of one or two actual chartered surveyors and several unqualified or inexperienced assistants who do the work. The partners must, of course, take the responsibility or indeed liability of those they employ, but in some trades individual accountability is sought (requiring individual qualifications), and hopefully one day this ethos will be extended to professionals in the industry. Whatever the charges, you can expect to receive a breakdown of the disbursements, such as travel, photographs, faxes, postage and local authority fees.

Inspections

Whether you want your designer to inspect the work on site is entirely up to you. The word 'supervise' seems to have gone out of fashion, by the way, and clauses in your terms of engagement now speak of 'inspecting', with the aim of 'guarding against deficiencies and defects as can be seen at these inspections'.

The idea being addressed in these caveats about the exclusion of continuous or exhaustive inspection of the work, is aimed at reducing the liability should things go wrong. With structural alterations, for example, the installation of a temporary support and beam would make for opportune inspection times, hence you might want to contract the builders into notifying your designer for inspection at specific stages during the work. General inspections left to the discretion of the adviser might be ill-timed or unnecessary.

Where your project is controlled by Building Regulations, inspections by the Building Control Officer will be necessary, and as the home-owner it is your responsibility to notify the Officer at certain stages. You can engage your builder in the task of notifying inspections on your behalf, but make sure you agree this in writing – it is a legal duty, and if you plan to contract it over to the builder, make sure it stays that way. I have heard of builders orating along the lines of, 'Well, I thought you were contacting the inspector, I carried on because I thought you wanted the job done quick...' and so on.

Some inspections are statutory in that you must request them, but others may be imposed by condition of approval. You should check with your Building Control Office if you are at all unsure about the stages at which they wish to be notified.

Professional Indemnity insurance

If you're employing a structural engineer or an architect as a consultant for your project, it is reasonable to expect them to have Professional Indemnity insurance. This indemnifies professionals from claims made against them, and in this way it is designed to protect them, not you, the client, or a third party. The good thing about such insurance is that it covers claims against the professional for negligence or omission made within the period of the insurance, irrespective of when the deed actually occurred. The bad news is that it costs professionals an arm and a leg in annual premiums, and this cost is represented in their fees.

One other oddity in this business is that sometimes it seems that professionals are specifically required by their insurers not to let on that they have PI cover, let alone for how much they are insured. If this is the case, you might be referred to the professional's broker when you ask for details of their cover. I can't imagine that it would happen often with home alterations, but professionals should be on their guard against being underinsured, although it is unlikely that your claim would be rejected because you, the claimant, would be able to utilise the full extent of their cover first. It is more likely that their defence costs would be split pro rata if the dispute ran into litigation.

PI insurance normally specifies the nature of the professional's undertakings; for example, an architectural designer would not normally have cover to prepare structural design calculations and undertake engineering design unless they were also qualified in this respect.

Negligence in respect of design failure may not present itself immediately after the project is complete. The Latent Damage Act means, however, that consultants still have some liability, and this makes it important for professionals to retain files for at least 15 years after the project has been undertaken. Claims can be made accordingly.

Planning Permission

For the most part, alteration and repair work is exempt from Planning Permission, even to the extent of replacing windows and doors or installing new windows, skylights, roof lights and solar panels – the latter so long as they don't extend significantly from the roof line. Over-roofing a flat roof with a pitched one, or adding dormer or bay windows, however, does extend up or out and add volume to your home, so these are treated as extensions. Permission may or may not be required, given the usual permitted development rights for extensions of this nature.

Re-covering your roof with a new material or cladding your walls is generally not subject to planning control. The exception to this is in Conservation Areas, National Parks and Areas of Outstanding Natural Beauty, or the Broads, where cladding requires permission. It is quite possible to destroy the character of an area with artificial stone or cladding which is why this has been made necessary.

Internal alterations

Internal alterations, such as removing internal walls, creating openings, repositioning stairs and so on, do not normally require Planning Permission. Listed buildings are the exception to this, and in these cases an application for Listed Building Consent should be made. These controls are also extended to other buildings that lie within the curtilage of a listed building, so they may also relate to outbuildings in the garden of your listed home.

Since it is a criminal offence to carry out work which needs consent in this respect without obtaining it, it is advisable to check with your Local Planning Office beforehand. Invariably a dedicated section of Conservation Officers exists within the local planning authority, acting as specialists for listed buildings and Conservation Area work.

Hard landscaping

The majority of hard-landscaping operations are exempt from planning controls, but once again, not all of them. To start with, you can hard-surface your entire garden if you so desire – and many of us, 'deranged' by garden makeover TV, are wont to do this, with decking, patios, concrete and so on.

There has always been, understandably, some confusion with driveways and hardstandings. Creating one does not in itself require Planning Permission, but often a dropped kerb on the highway is needed, and installing one of these does. This is the vehicle crossover, the bit where the public footpath between your home and the road has to be crossed and the kerb lowered, even if no footpath exists and the space is simply a verge.

The same applies if you plan to widen your driveway access onto a classified road, such as a trunk road. Work like this can have an effect on highway safety, and will be dependent on your receiving Planning Permission. The local authority Highways Office will be able to advise you of the status of your access road in this respect.

Returning to the subject of decks and patios and our increased interest in structural gardening, elevated patios and decks that might, for example, overcome a steeply sloping garden by extending out from your home above ground level, can require Planning Permission. This is down to individual situations and the merits of each one, but if you are left with an undercroft area of some usable space, then the chances are it will be treated as an extension or a garden building, and thus be subject to the usual controls or permitted development rules.

Garden walls, fences and gates

Some controls do exist for these, in that height limitations apply, beyond which Planning Permission is needed. Next to a highway, the cut-off point for exemption is 1 m high, but otherwise it is 2 m, which explains why fence panels are made 1.8 m high, or more likely the other way around.

In Conservation Areas as a separate matter, Conservation Area Consent is needed for the removal of some buildings, fences, walls and gates. Again, this is in the case of the latter, which are over 1 m high when adjacent to a highway or public open space, and elsewhere 2 m for consent to be required, even though in this instance you are taking them down. This also applies to railings, and enables the planning authority to exercise controls over the demolition of features they believe to be intrinsic to the special nature of the area.

Demolition of buildings

On the subject of demolition, sheds and garages less than 50 cu m in volume can be taken down without permission, unless you reside in a Conservation Area, or they are listed. If the building has become dangerous, regardless of its size Planning Permission can be overridden by the Building Act procedures under Sections 77 and 78 regarding Dangerous Structures. These are normally administered by the authority's Building Control Officers and structural engineers. If the building has been left in such a state of repair or has met with some unfortunate event that has made it a threat to public safety, you could be required to demolish it. A notice to this effect will be served on you; the notice negates the need to acquire consent.

Fuel storage tanks

The task of installing new fuel storage tanks is often subject to Planning Permission, largely I think because they are ugly (the fuel tanks, not the planners). Large oil tanks for storing heating oil with a capacity of more than 3,500 l, and those that are higher than 3 m above ground level require planning permission. Unfortunately, it doesn't end there, because controls are also introduced if the oil tank is positioned closer to the highway than the nearest part of your home, or whenever the tank will be closer than 20 m to the highway – again, highways are defined in the sense of public roads, footpaths, bridlepaths and public rights of way. With Building Regulation controls on the positioning of such tanks away from homes and the need to locate them in accessible areas for refuelling, they often fall into this category and Planning Permission is needed.

LPG tanks of any size or description also need Planning Permission, regardless of their location.

Permitted Development Rights

If your home has not been altered or extended since 1948, when national planning controls were first introduced, you may have a certain amount of freedom over alterations that would need Planning Permission. Permitted Development Rights are quantifiable in terms of volume, depending on your home's location and whether or not it is terraced. These rights can, however, be removed by planning conditions, placed perhaps on the home when it was built, or by Article 4 directives. The latter are broad-banded areas that have an acknowledged need for extra controls and are most commonly found in Conservation Areas.

As I've said, the vast majority of alteration and repair work is not subject to Planning Permission, but there are exceptions. Over-roofing a flat roof with a pitched one is development in planning terms, as it adds to the volume of your home, but whether you need to acquire Planning Permission for it will depend upon its size and your allowance of Permitted Development Rights.

Permitted Development Rights also vary in quota from a roof attached to your home to a roof on a detached garage or garden building. The volumes and sizes for permitted development in all these cases are given in the table that follows. Every property has Permitted

Development Rights, but they are expendable: once you have used them up they cannot be renewed without demolishing something. In a few cases Permitted Development Rights may be removed by conditions of previous Planning Permissions, in an effort to exert greater control over development. Your local authority planning office will advise you of your Permitted Development Rights on request, although they will need to know some information about the scale of your proposal and any previous additions to the property.

A home that has not been extended before might still have Permitted Development Rights, which would allow you to extend without needing Planning Consent. The law changes regularly as to what constitutes permitted development, and you should always check with your local Planning Authority and apply for a Lawful Development Certificate for your particular project.

Under the Town and Country Planning Act 1990 (General Development Order), current guidelines for Permitted Development in England and Wales are as follows (variations in Scotland under the Town and Country Planning (General Permitted Development) (Scotland) Order 1992 are shown in brackets):

Porches:
- of no more than 3 sq m ground area (measured externally)

- and no more than 3 m height above ground

● and at least 2 m from a public highway (which means a public road, public footpath, public bridleway or byway)

Bay window extensions which are:
1) no higher than the highest part of the existing house, **or:**
   when within 2 m of your property boundary, the extension is in no part higher than 4 m
2) when it would extend the existing roof

General cases
2a) no bigger than 15 per cent of the existing house in volume or 70 cu m (Scotland: 20 per cent or 24 sq m floor area), whichever is the greater, and definitely no bigger than 115 cu m in volume (Scotland: 30 sq m floor area).

2b) **Changing a flat roof to a pitched roof** (over-roofing) or extending the roof (such as by dormer windows)

● The roof extension will add less than 50 cu m to the volume of the house

● The roof extension is to a roof slope which does not face the highway

● The roof extension does not increase the height of the roof

Special cases
are terraced houses and also properties in the following designated areas: **Area of Outstanding Natural Beauty, National Park, Conservation Area, the Norfolk and Suffolk Broads.**

3a) The extension is no bigger than 10 per cent of the existing house in volume (Scotland: in floor area) or 50 cu m (Scotland: 16 sq m floor area), whichever is the greater, and definitely no bigger than 115 cu m in volume (Scotland: 30 square metres floor area).

3b) An extension to the roof, such as a dormer window, is only exempt in the case of terraced houses, providing it is no bigger than 40 cu m in volume. **Note:** In the other special areas listed above, Planning Consent will be required.

Note: In all cases, volume is measured externally and includes roof space.

4) That no part of your extension is nearer to a public highway than any part of the existing house, unless it is at least 20 m away from your finished house (as extended).
Public Highway definitions are as given under Porches. Watch out for public footpaths within 20 m - that is **65 ft 6 in!**

5) No more than 50 per cent of the total area of land around your original house has been built on by additions or other buildings. (In Scotland this has been reduced to a maximum of 30 per cent.)

6) There are NO Permitted Development Rights for extensions to **listed buildings**.

7) No Article 4 directive or Condition of Permission is in force on your property,

removing Permitted Development Rights (these are sometimes used in Conservation Areas, where greater control is needed).

Conservation Areas are defined as 'areas of special architectural or historic interest, the character or appearance of which it is desirable to preserve or enhance'. They are designated by the controlling local authority in consultation with parish councils, local amenity societies and the general public in the area.

Areas of Special Control exist in some parts of the UK, which although too small to be considered as Conservation Areas, have been designated so to protect the architectural or historical value of the area. Permitted Development Rights will be affected.

Farmhouses are not usually considered as being domestic dwellings for planning purposes.

Extensions to council houses will also require the consent of the local authority Housing Department. Even recently sold council houses may carry restrictive covenants to this effect.

Because the first Town and Country Planning Act came in on 1 July 1948, anything built on or after that date in the way of extensions, porches, garages, etc. counts towards your permitted development quota, and if your property has had any add-ons since 1 July 1948, then you might not have any

rights left at all. If this is the case, you may only recover Permitted Development Rights by demolishing some or all of the old buildings.

Notification

In England and Wales, the local Planning Authority will notify your neighbours of your proposals, either by letter, advertisement in the local press or by a notice displayed nearby. In Scotland it is the responsibility of the applicant to consult his neighbours and submit their signed comments. Forms for this purpose are usually acquired with the planning application forms and should be returned completed when the application is made. In the former, interested parties have a couple of weeks to lodge their objections if they have any. It is therefore, sometimes beneficial to show them your plans and consult with them beforehand.

A number of people and organisations are consulted in the planning process – parish councils, environmental groups, etc. – and it takes some time for all comments to be collected. If there are any objections, it does not necessarily mean that your scheme will be refused. It does mean that it may be presented at a planning committee or sub-committee meeting, and will thus be decided by councillors rather than by the delegated powers of planning officers. In reality, the case officer will prepare a short report and make a recommendation, which, more often than not, will be adopted. You should be entitled to see any such report together with any consultee's comments, but you will not be sent them automatically, so make enquiries and ask.

In Northern Ireland, planning applications are made to the Department of the Environment for Northern Ireland, who have six divisional offices. These offices carry out the planning function in place of the local authorities, although they do consult with them.

For a full and definitive statement of the law concerning planning, consultation should be made to the relevant current statutory instrument.

You can obtain written confirmation of your exemption from permission in the form of a Lawful Development Certificate or simply a letter, which should be included in your home logbook. You will need to produce this letter should you sell or re-mortgage your home.

Making a planning application

You can obtain the standard application forms for Planning Permission from your local authority, along with details of the current fees. The forms need to be submitted in multiple copies along with your plans or details, and on receipt of them you should be written to with a date by which the application should be decided. This is a statutory eight-week date, but it can be extended on with your consent. A Planning Officer will normally visit your home to see where the proposal is sited on it and how it relates to the neighbourhood in general and nearby homes in particular.

During the first few weeks, neighbours as well as other local organisations and authorities will have the opportunity to comment on your proposal, and these views will be collated and taken into consideration. If there are objections, the decision is likely to be referred to the next available planning committee or sub-committee meeting, and the dates for these can be obtained. To keep informed of your application's progress throughout its course, you can contact your Planning Case Officer.

Listed Building Consent

If you are fortunate to live in a home that is listed, you may well need to apply for Listed Building Consent to carry out alterations or repairs on it. These consents are required to protect the architectural and historic value that listed buildings have, and are bespoke to each building in their requirements – which is why it is difficult to publish advice on what they may or may not require from you. The system of listing was only introduced in 1950, and grades are given to each property. In England and Wales, Grades I, II* and II apply, and in Scotland and Northern Ireland Grades A, B and C apply, far more logically and sensibly.

If your home was built before 1700 and any part of it is original, it should be listed, and a percentage of homes built between then and 1840 are also covered. After that it becomes a little rare, and after 1945 it becomes extremely rare. If you are still not certain whether your home is listed, you can telephone the Listed Buildings

Information Service or your local Planning Authority, who hold a copy of the list. Some half a million buildings are on the list, of which over 90 per cent are recorded as Grade II. If you're fortunate enough to own a Grade I or II* property in England, you may be eligible for grant aid with any major repairs from English Heritage – in Northern Ireland the Ulster Architectural Society, in Scotland Historic Scotland, and in Wales Cadw (meaning keep) have equivalent roles to English Heritage.

Local authorities are also able to provide grants for alteration and repair, and are not restricted to grades of buildings but free to use their discretion. Grants can also be used in Conservation Areas or other special areas where owners are trying to preserve or enhance the character of their homes.

If you're planning to carry out alteration work or demolition to your home, and the authority consider it should be listed, you could potentially find yourself served with a Building Preservation Notice, which is sort of like an emergency temporary listing, effective for six months.

Whether you need to make an application for consent is entirely dependent on the local planning authority's view on your proposals. If they consider that the work would alter the building in a way that affects its character internally or externally, consent is likely to be needed. The only way to be sure is to ask. Most authorities have dedicated conservation officers to administer these applications.

In extreme cases of neglect, the authority is able to serve a 'repairs notice' on the owner of a listed building, requiring them to carry out specified repairs. These notices give two months for the work to be carried out. Failing to do so could leave the authority to carry out repairs themselves and recover costs from you; ultimately, if the property is neglected to its detriment, they may compulsorily purchase it from you – as my residing authority did with the local windmill.

Building Regulations

Building Regulations impose minimum technical standards on some alteration and repair work, with the aim of ensuring a minimum level of health and safety and energy conservation. The detailed requirements are contained in Parts, for which Approved Documents give technical advice on how to comply.

Alterations

Most alteration work is controlled under the Building Regulations, and for this work you will need to submit an application to your Building Control authority and seek their approval. Alas, the list of alteration projects under control seems to grow with each passing year, although using recognised tradesmen who are able to certify their own work will give you exemption in some cases.

Structural alterations

Starting with the obvious, structural alterations can be described as any work that alters part of your home's structure, whether it be the roof, walls or floor. Cutting joists or rafters to form an opening for a stair or rooflight is a structural alteration, as is cutting a hole in a loadbearing wall for a window or door. External walls are loadbearing, but some internal walls can also be loadbearing, and once cut through or demolished, would need to be replaced with a lintel or beam to carry the load. If your alteration involves removing part or all of a loadbearing wall, you will need to make an application under the Building Regulations. (See page 53 for what to look for when deciding whether a wall is loadbearing or not.) Removing a non-loadbearing wall isn't a structural alteration.

Taking down part of your chimney or cutting back a chimney breast can also be described as a structural alteration if you have some retained structure above it to be supported. In other words, if you remove the ground-floor chimney breast but leave the first floor section, you will need to support it somewhere around first-floor level. Or if you remove the chimney breasts in all the rooms but leave the chimney coming out of the roof, you will need to support it somewhere in the attic. Electing to remove the chimney from the top down (starting with the pots) solves everything. Yes, you will have a hole in the roof to make good, but you will not alter the structure of your home in doing so.

For the Building Control Officer checking your work, there are two key elements in structural alterations. The first is to ensure that you install a method of support to the structure that is adequate and can safely carry and transmit the loads down. This can sometimes need to be proved by structural calculations, but often it can be judged by inspection alone. It isn't uncommon to find builders or homeowners choosing to install an oversized beam, rather than engaging the services of an engineer to calculate a more accurately sized one. If you do choose to do this, at least make sure that your Building Control Officer knows what size beam you plan to install and agrees it beforehand.

The second element is to consider whether the alterations have adversely affected your safety from fire. Knocking down a hallway wall and rendering your staircase open-plan to the living room will create 'inner rooms' upstairs. Inner rooms are rooms that require windows you can escape from should a fire break out in the outer room, preventing you from getting out the usual way.

Repairs

Most repair work is exempt from Building Regulations, but not all of it, notably underpinning, which has been controlled since 1985. Repairs that are extensive enough to involve replacing elements like roofs or drainage systems are usually controlled under the regulations as 'replacements' rather than 'repairs'. It is important to check with your own local authority Building Control office for confirmation of exemption, and to obtain it in writing. The lists on page 28 give an indication of what is subject to control and what is exempted.

Examples of work subject to Building Regulations control:

○ Forming or altering a stairwell

○ Re-covering the roof with a heavier or lighter roof material

○ Installing a new window or door in an external wall

○ Forming an opening in an internal loadbearing wall

○ Underpinning

○ Removing any lower part of a chimney

● Installing a new boiler *

○ Installing heating oil or LPG fuel storage tanks/cylinders*

○ Making a sewer connection*

● Installing new drainage above or below ground*

○ Extending and adding electrical power and lighting circuits* (possibly from 2004 – Part P)

○ Replacing windows and doors*

● Cavity wall insulation (regulated by formal notices from approved installers)

* Work of this nature carried out by an 'approved person' who can self-certify its compliance with the Regulations does not need an application.

Examples of work not subject to Building Regulations control:

● Forming an opening in a non-loadbearing wall

● Repairing damaged drainage

● Re-covering a roof with a material of a similar weight

● Re-laying floor boarding

● Rewiring existing electrical circuits

● Adding RCD protection to existing electrical circuits

● Installing water softeners or limescale reducers

● Adding external cold-water supply taps

● Insulating the loft

● Repairing broken or damaged timbers

● Repointing brickwork

● Replacing glass panes

● Replacing fascia, barge and soffit boards.

● Replacing sanitaryware (connected to the existing drainage system)

There will always be grey areas as to what constitutes an application. For instance, boarding out the whole loft space would not in itself amount to a structural alteration, but if your reason for doing it was to heavily load it with storage, an application to justify the loadbearing ability of the ceiling joists might be necessary.

Repair work is generally exempt from Building Regulations, with the exception of underpinning. Repairs can mean replacing drainpipes, rebuilding damaged walls or parts of a roof, but should they become extensive an application may be required. 'Extensive' could mean replacing the drainage system with a new one, or taking the roof off and constructing a new one. Check with your local Building Control Authority if in doubt, and acquire written confirmation. Some authorities operate a system for recording these 'exempt enquiries', and a written response is always best.

Design self-certification

Present in Scotland only, this system is extended to Structural Design Certificates, which can be submitted by either full or corporate members of the Institute of Civil Engineers or the Chartered Institute of Structural Engineers as a statement of compliance. They are, in effect, self-certifying the structural design of the scheme. A 'supporting statement' must be submitted with them as to the stability of the building, and a new design certificate must be submitted for any amendments affecting the structure that are made later. Plans showing the structural design are still required to be submitted for reference showing the conditions that the design is based on,

for instance loadbearing support of internal walls, bearing capacity of subsoil assumed. Conditions such as these can then be verified on site by inspection once the work starts.

The self-certification idea started in Scotland with the case of qualified structural designers who are able to submit certificates for work such as structural alterations as a way of demonstrating compliance. The procedure basically says, 'I'm a qualified person in this area, I know what I'm doing and take full responsibility for my work, so I don't need to have it checked, thank you very much.'

When the scheme was first launched it was intended that it would spread to other professions in the industry, but it never did, because nobody could agree on a regime.

Building Regulation applications
Full Plans

If you would like the full details of your work checked and approved before you start, a Full Plans Application is for you, where drawings, and in some cases structural calculations, should be submitted for consideration. Building Regulations work to a statutory five-week date (which may be extended with your consent to two months), and the authority may write to you, setting out a list of defects or amendments to the plans required before approval. Alternatively, they may simply make these points the subject of a Conditional Approval. Either result should be addressed before work starts, to avoid problems on site.

LOCAL AUTHORITY BUILDING CONTROL

FULL PLANS SUBMISSION

The Building Act 1984
The Building Regulations 2000

Building Regulations
Plan Number:

This Full Plans notice conforms to the Building Regulations 2000 and may be
used to deposit Full Plans with any Local Authority in England and Wales.

*This form is to be filled in by the person who intends to carry out building work or agent. If the form is unfamiliar
please read the notes which follow or consult your local Building Control office.*

1 **Applicant's details** (see note 1)
Name:
Address:
Postcode: Tel: Fax: email:

2 **Agent's details** (if applicable)
Name:
Address:
Postcode: Tel: Fax: email:

3 **Location of building to which work relates**
Address:
Postcode: Tel: Fax: email:

4 **Proposed Work** (see note 5)
Description:
Is the proposed work or any part of it subject to Partnering or a current LANTAC approval?   YES ☐ NO ☐

5 **Use of building**
1. If new building or extension please state proposed use:
2. If existing building state present use:
3. Is the building to be put, or intended to be put, to a use which is designated
for the purpose of the Fire Precautions Act 1971 (see note 6)?   YES ☐ NO ☐

6 **Conditions** (see note 7)
Do you consent to the plans being passed subject to conditions where appropriate?   YES ☐ NO ☐

7 **Fees** (see Guidance Note of Fees for information) N.B. When fees are based on estimated cost of the
work a written estimate of the total cost of the work shown on the plans must be provided.
Plan fee £   + VAT at 17½%   Total £   Estimate enclosed YES ☐ NO ☐

8 **Additional Information:**

9 **Statement**
This notice is given in relation to the building work as described, is submitted in accordance with Regulation
12(2)(b) and is accompanied by the appropriate fee. I understand that further fees will normally be payable
following the first inspection by the local authority.

BUILDING
CONTROL   Name: Signature: Date:

If you do intend to submit your own plans, it is quite likely that unless you are familiar with current Building Regulations and construction, they will need to be amended. If you have some faith in your builder's knowledge and abilities, you may wish to avoid a Full Plans Application under the Building Regulations and submit a Building Notice (not available in Scotland).

Building Notice

This is a statement of your intention to do work and comply with the requirements of the regulations, and requires no plans or design information to be submitted. It gives your Building Control Officer 48 hours notice of your intention to start the job. The officer will inspect the work at various stages on notification by you or your builder, and will advise you of any problems drawn to their attention.

There is a certain element of risk with the Building Notice method, because you do not have the benefit of an approved plan to work to, and the Building Control Officer may not always be able to predict and warn you of any problems ahead of you. Consequently it is only advisable to adopt this procedure after discussing the scheme in detail with your builder and Building Control Officer, and then only if you are satisfied that they can agree on the details before each stage of the work.

The fees for both procedures are usually identical, although Building Notice fees are often paid 100 per cent on submission, and Full Plans 25 per cent on submission and 75 per cent on commencement. Building Control

authorities set their own fees, which thus vary from one authority to another.

Building Warrant (Scotland)

In Scotland you must obtain a Building Warrant before starting work – it is not possible to build at your risk by starting work in advance of receiving the Warrant. In lieu of the Approved Documents, the Scottish Regulations are documented by the Technical Standards.

Unauthorised work

Until the early 1990s the dangers of carrying out unauthorised alterations and repairs were scarcely noticeable, and a great many projects that should have been the subject of Building Regulation control went without it. Completion Certificates were introduced about then to provide proof that not only had an application been made for the work, but that it had been inspected and was carried out satisfactorily. One court case changed things even further, when new home-owners successfully sued their conveyancing solicitors for failing to tell them they were buying a home with unauthorised work.

As the owner of the home has liability for any contraventions it may have, this liability is passed on with the home to its new owners. Home-owners have found that when they now come to sell their homes, unauthorised work from the past comes to light and has to be corrected; the buyer's solicitors will not risk conveying a home with unauthorised work on it, and effectively the property is blighted until it is regularised – rather unjust if the

LOCAL AUTHORITY BUILDING CONTROL

BUILDING NOTICE

The Building Act 1984
The Building Regulations 2000

Building Regulations
Plan Number:

This **Building notice conforms to the Building Regulations 2000 and may be used for submissions to any Local Authority in England and Wales.**

This form is to be filled in by the person who intends to carry out building work or agent. If the form is unfamiliar please read the notes which follow or consult your local Building Control office.

---

1   **Applicant's details** (see note 1)
Name:
Address:
Postcode: Tel: Fax: email:

2   **Agent's details** (if applicable)
Name:
Address:
Postcode: Tel: Fax: -   email:

3   **Location of building to which work relates**
Address:
Postcode: Tel: Fax: email:

4   **Proposed Work** (see note 6)
Description:
Is the proposed work or any part of it subject to Partnering or a current LANTAC approval?   YES ☐ NO ☐
Number of storeys in building:
Anticipated date of commencement (see note 7)

5   **Use of building**
1. If new building or extension please state proposed use:
2. If existing building state present use:

6   **Fees** (see SEPARATE Guidance Note on Fees for information)
Building notice fee £   plus VAT at 17½%   Total £
Total floor area of any new building or extension:
Estimate of *total* cost of work shown on plans where they are subject to fees in accordance with
Schedule 3 £   excluding VAT.
N.B.   The appropriate fee should be submitted with this notice.

7   **Additional Information:**

8   **Statement**
This notice is given in relation to the building work as described, and is submitted in accordance with Regulation 12(2)(a).

BUILDING
CONTROL

Name: Signature: Date:

---

offending work was done by previous owners and wasn't revealed when you bought, but there it stands.

If you fall into the bracket of needing to apply for a Regularisation Certificate yourself, you need to understand that these certificates are only available for work carried out under the present 'style' of Building Regulations introduced in November 1985. You need to state this on the application form.

This system has been exercised a great deal since the Millennium, and I don't believe it was foreseen just how many unauthorised alterations and repairs had taken place or what a major role Building Control would play in home conveyancing. Certificates are best applied for well in advance of any transaction, particularly when remedial work has to be done to bring the job into compliance, because delays during property sales are delays of the most frustrating and expensive kind.

Cowboy builders

Building Control has expanded out in recent years from its original health and safety interests into a broad spectrum of controls that include providing access for people with disabilities into buildings, and reducing carbon emissions from buildings through energy efficiency. There are now plans to add requirements for supplying broadband telecommunication cables to homes, final confirmation that whichever government is in power will use the vehicle of Building Regulations for whatever purpose they see fit.

The one thing it hasn't been used for yet is to control the quality of workmanship in building. It is difficult to understand but the fact is that the regulations offer you no protection from cowboy builders. If you employ one to work on your behalf, then you take responsibility for what they do. This sad truth is enhanced by the fact that the system makes the home-owner legally responsible for the work on their property, and it is you that would be prosecuted for contraventions, not the builder. Until the day arrives when builders have to be registered and monitored with a national body and authorities have the power to remove that registration, nobody is safe from rogue traders.

The Party Wall, Etc. Act 1996
Party walls

These are the separating walls within semi-detached and terraced homes that are shared with your neighbour and with whom joint ownership exists.

What alterations and repairs are covered?

Most alteration and repair work will not be covered by the act, but there are exceptions when you will need to comply with it. To some extent it is a matter of degree when considering how much a party wall will be affected by your project. Installing a beam like a RSJ, with one end bearing on it, for example, is not covered; nor is fixing a chimney support bracket to a party wall. If you are on the other hand proposing to rebuild part of the wall or underpin it, then you will be covered by the act and will need to observe its procedures.

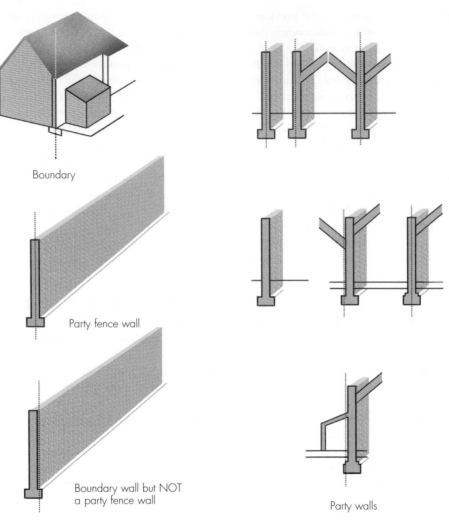

Boundary

Party fence wall

Boundary wall but NOT
a party fence wall

Party walls

Party walls and party fence walls are defined by the Party Wall, Etc. Act.

In fact, underpinning work can be covered even when it isn't the party wall you're underpinning. This is because it is the 'Party Wall, Etc. Act 1996' and not just the 'Party Wall Act 1996'. The etcetera bit is excavations near boundaries, and near can mean as

distant as up to 6 m; within 3 m you are definitely under the act's control, and between 3 and 6 m, it depends on how deep your underpinning is. The problem here is that 'deep' is usually the point of it. If the depth takes you down beneath a 45° line of spread from the bottom of your neighbour's home, this could be covered. There should not, however, be a problem if the work is being done in bays and appropriately sequenced. Underpinning has to proceed carefully for the sake of your own home, and the by-product of this should always safeguard adjacent property.

Notifying your neighbours

Notification can't simply be verbal, it has to be done in writing, but obviously you should talk to your neighbours as well. The notice should contain your present name and address, as well as that of your contractors. It should state that it is being given in accordance with the Party Wall, Etc. Act 1996 and give full details with a copy of your plans of what you intend to do and when you intend to start the work.

If the property next door is let, you will also have to notify the landlord as well as the occupiers as tenants. If the place is empty, you may post the notice somewhere prominent on the building.

The act is more about giving notice of your intentions, than actually asking for permission. As already mentioned, the notice must be given at least two months beforehand, and any response must come within 14 days. If neighbours don't respond at all, or if they respond with objections, then surveyors may be needed on both sides to reach an agreement. Unfortunately, the act does say that if they haven't responded a 'dispute' has arisen, and so for this reason alone it pays to talk to your neighbours and agree the details informally before serving the notice on them. In the case of subsidence

underpinning it would be neighbourly to keep them informed, as their side may be the next to move.

One other benefit of telling neighbours first is that if they agree, you don't have to wait for two months before doing the work.

Party wall disputes and payments

If you and your neighbour have a disagreement about the work you are proposing, in the first instance you might want to ask your designer, structural engineer or builder if there is any other way of doing it. The chances are that there is another method that your neighbour can live with, and you don't really want to be paying for a party wall surveyor if you can sort it out yourself.

If you can't agree and a surveyor is appointed, their task is to draw up a Party Wall Award. This is a legally binding agreement of the work that is to take place on a certain date/s with rights of access to their side if necessary, although it shouldn't be necessary unless you are underpinning the wall. The award should also record the state of the adjacent walls, so if there is any claim against damage arising from the proposals it can be fairly assessed.

If your neighbours still do not agree with the award details, they have 14 days to appeal to the County Court. I suppose the biggest hurdle that this act has to clear is with the neighbour who just refuses to play, doesn't respond, doesn't appoint their own surveyor, and so on. In these situations you can appoint a surveyor for them so that the

TYPICAL LOADS FOR HOMES			
	KILONEWTONS PER SQUARE METRE		
	DEAD	LIVE	TOTAL
Timber studwork internal wall			
covered with plasterboard each side	0.40		0.40
covered with lathe & plaster each side	0.60		0.60
Timber studwork external wall			
covered with plain tiles outside	0.90		0.90
Brick internal wall			
102 mm thick with plaster both sides	2.50		2.50
215 mm thick with plaster both sides	4.70		4.70
330 mm thick with plaster both sides	7.00		7.00
Brick/block external cavity wall			
102 mm brick/ 100 mm block plastered inside	3.30		3.30
Timber floors	0.50	1.5	2.0
Flat roofs			
built-up felt covered with chippings	0.85	0.75	1.45
Pitched roofs			
covered with concrete tiles	0.65	0.75	1.40
covered with clay plain tiles	0.75	0.75	1.50
covered with slates	0.45	0.75	1.20
Roof void and ceiling	0.25	0.25	0.50

procedure goes ahead, but it should not be the same one that you are using.

If you are the sole person benefiting from this work and the one who is proposing to have it done, then you have the total bill to pay; you can't share it. Clearly, though, if you are underpinning the party wall, both sides will benefit and both should pay.

If you overlook the notification procedure, your neighbours can seek a court injunction or other legal redress, requiring you to stop work.

Structural designing
The weight of your home

When structural designers calculate the load to elements of your home, such as new beams, they use accepted values for certain parts. Standard weights that are converted to loads (by multiplying them against the force of gravity) are made up of two parts – dead and imposed. Dead loads are those applied by the weight of the materials your home is made of. Weights are available from the manufacturers for current materials, but more often, accepted 'standard' weights are used, and these are published in British Standards. See the table on page 38 for examples.

For a designer to assess the dead load in total, however, the area over which it applies must be measured, and this can be done either by running around your home with a tape measure, or by measurement from scale drawings.

Given gravity at the usual rate of 9.81 m per second, a typical timber floor structure exerts a dead load of 0.5 kn (kilonewtons) per square metre, made up from the weight of the floor joists, floorboards, ceiling plasterboard and finish. You might better be able to visualise this load in terms of weight: half a kilonewton in force roughly equals 50 kg in weight – 110 lb, or 50 bags of sugar.

Imposed or live loads are those applied by our furniture, the weather and us. A floor in a standard home has an accepted imposed load of 1.5 kn per square metre, equating roughly to 150 kg. An average adult could represent half of that, leaving the same again for the furniture – all equally spread over every square metre of floor. These figures are also published by British Standards and have become what is considered as the accepted allowance. Of course not all elements of your home will have live loads: an internal partition, for example, may only have its own self-weight if it doesn't support a floor, ceiling or roof. Figures for both types of load are expressed over a square metre so that they can be multiplied against the total area to determine the whole load.

In the case of a beam, this whole load, when distributed evenly along its length, is known as the UDL (uniformly distributed load) and is expressed per metre length. When multiplied to the effective length of the beam, it becomes the total load on that beam, and this figure can be compared to the safe working load. Beams are usually designed, however, by calculating their maximum bending moment, the maximum shear stress and the maximum deflection on them. If they meet each of these three conditions without failing, they can safely be used.

WEIGHT OF BUILDING MATERIALS

Pitched roof materials

Clay tiles	70 kg/sq m
Concrete tiles	60 kg/sq m
Welsh slates	25–40 kg/sq m
Corrugated plastic sheeting	5 kg/sq m

Flat roof materials

Asphalt, two layers 19 mm thick	42 kg/sq m
Bitumen felts faced with chippings	4 kg/sq m
Lead sheet 2.5 mm thick	30 kg/sq m

Wall materials

Blockwork, lightweight aerated per 25 mm thick	15 kg/sq m
Blockwork, concrete per 25 mm thick	55 kg/sq m
Brickwork per 25 mm thick	55 kg/sq m
Plaster, two coats gypsum 12 mm thick	22 kg/sq m
Rendering cement and sand 12 mm thick	30 kg/sq m

Floors

Timber (softwood)	590 kg/cu m
Plywood 19 mm thick	12 kg/sq m
Concrete	2400 kg/sq m
Linoleum 3 mm thick	6 kg/sq m
Concrete 50 mm thick paving stones	120 kg/sq m
Floor screed 50 mm thick	120 kg/sq m
Water (in tanks allow for 1 tonne per cu m)	1000 kg/cu m
Steel	7850 kg/cu m

MAXIMUM BENDING STRESS IN BEAMS	
Softwoods	
C16 grade	5.3 n/mm sq
C24 grade	7.5 n/mm sq
Hardwoods	
Iroko, jarrah, teak, English oak	10 n/mm sq
Keruing	10 n/mm sq
Greenheart	20.5 n/mm sq

The maximum bending moment

The maximum bending moment is calculated by formula, depending on the pattern of the load, which includes the total weight, the span of the beam and a constant. It is expressed as kilonewton metres (kn m). It is a statement of the limits of bending for a beam that can be compared against an allowable limit. This is the primary design factor for all beams.

The allowable limit is the permitted maximum bending moment, and this is also calculated by formula and employs a factor known as the 'section modulus' of the beam. If you had a rectangular timber beam, the section modulus is calculated by its breadth multiplied by the depth squared, divided by six. When the shape varies, the section modulus varies. With RSJs the figures are quoted in published Steel Design Tables.

In a simply supported beam with two end bearings and a UDL applied, the formula for calculating the actual maximum (worst case) bending moment, is the total load multiplied by the effective span of the beam, divided by eight. The same formula can be expressed as the UDL multiplied by the effective span squared, divided by eight. A different formula exists for each different loading condition, such as where point loads occur, changes in the UDL are present, or where the bearing positions differ.

The maximum shear stress

In a simply supported beam with two end bearings and a UDL applied, the maximum shear occurs near the bearings and amounts to half the total load. The shear stress is expressed in newtons per sq mm, and is compared to the known shear stress of the material of the beams.

The maximum deflection

You won't be surprised to hear that the formula for calculating deflection is complex. It includes values for the elasticity of the material and the moment of inertia for the beam shape and size, the total load applied, the span of the beam and a few constants thrown in for good measure. Actual deflection is therefore individual to every situation.

In spite of all this science, deflection is fairly obvious. When a joist or beam is deflecting a lot you can see it; on a floor you can feel it. It's the spring when you jump up and down in the centre.

With floors, the deflection should not exceed 14 mm at its worse case because of the risk of finishings being damaged, meaning that a plaster ceiling will crack. I doubt that you would want a floor with this much bounce to it.

You won't be astounded to learn that the industry has been employing computer programs to take some of the hard work and pocket calculator-thumping out of the job. Like any computer program, however, the engineer has to take responsibility for the information entered, and in this case that is the loads, their pattern and the effective span of the beam. Get those wrong and the answer is wrong – perhaps disastrously wrong. To my knowledge there are no computers that can scan your home, measure and assess the loads for you, so it looks as though we are stuck with structural engineers for some time to come.

The strength of wood

As anyone who has ever worked with wood will tell you, the strength can vary tremendously from one species to another and from one piece to another. Because of this, a classification has existed for grouping timber together according to its graded strength. The scheme has changed a bit over recent years, from GS and SS grades to a simple 1–9 scale at which the softest species were at the bottom and the hardest were at the top. SC3 and SC4 aligned with the old GS and SS codes respectively. I liked this system – it was easy to understand, and this presumably was the reason why it was quickly abolished. Currently we are using an obscure C prefix code number for grading that indicates C16 as the

standard grade structural timber (SC3) and C24 as the higher grade structural timber (SC4).

What haven't changed are the measurements of strength themselves, expressed as stresses, the overriding one being the permitted stress limit for bending of the timber parallel to its grain. In other words, a timber beam.

Dry stress-grading

Timber has a lot of moisture left in it when it ceases to be a tree, and this takes time to come out. If we were to use newly felled green timber in our homes straight away, its drying-out process would undoubtedly cause it to twist, split and generally warp beyond all recognition. In 1995 new standards for drying timber before its use in buildings were introduced, and were accompanied by a new mark so we could all see that it complied.

The mark to look for must include the word 'DRY' or the initials 'KD', meaning kiln-dried. They indicate that the moisture content was less than 20 per cent when it was stress-graded at the sawmill. Higher than 20 per cent attracts the mark 'WET', which is astoundingly simple. What it doesn't tell you, of course, is whether the timber has been stored outside in the rain at the builder's merchants for the last two months and is saturated when you buy it. Timber always needs to be kept covered and dry, and in this way it is stronger and will deflect less, it will be more resistant to fungal attack, it will be more stable and easier to paint and treat, and, very importantly, it will weigh noticeably less.

CHAPTER 3

Builders or DIY

Because you've gone to the trouble of reading this book – for which I'm extremely grateful – it would be easy to fall into the trap of assuming that you are either a professional home-owner or builder. I sometimes think that the government has everybody in mind for one of these two categories, but I can tell you that if they do, they have it wrong. There exists a tremendous variation on the scale of those undertaking home-improvement works. I say 'the' scale, but it's probably more fair to consider two scales, one for home-owners and one for builders.

At one end of the home-owner scale we have the diligent DIY kind who researches the best materials and practises thoroughly before tackling anything, and then makes a better job at it than most professionals – often because it takes them twice as long. At the other end we have the DIY enthusiast who can render his home a dangerous structure over the course of a bank holiday weekend and threaten the homes of nearby neighbours into the bargain. It happens surprisingly often. The odd person has been known to carry out internal alterations with a chainsaw, bringing on the partial collapse of his home. On a few occasions people have burned down their roofs and sometimes their neighbour's roofs with a blowtorch, while attempting to burn off old paint from a fascia board, on one notable occasion, the latter being a new owner's unfortunate way of introducing himself to the neighbours.

Then you have a whole category in itself, comprising people who just can't resist salvaging materials for long-term storage or, worse, some indescribable 'home improvement'. How do you legislate for people wandering into Building Control Offices and announcing that they've found some wood and were wondering what they could do with it – and not accepting 'How about a bonfire?' for an answer. I don't mean to be disparaging, because I know there are TV shows based on people using scrapyard junk to build things, but I question whether they should be using these methods to build their homes.

Builders

Builders of course have their own range, equally if not more diverse, and for the home-owner the challenge is to work out where your builder fits into this range before he starts work on your prize possession. Builders can at best be diligent craftsmen with exacting standards and a strong reputation to work to, or at worst conmen trying to separate vulnerable people from their money in return for damaging their homes. Somewhere in the middle of these extremes you have most builders, who range from fairly competent and professional to fairly incompetent and unknowledgeable.

In short, finding a builder is a lottery, and if Building Control Offices were ever permitted to publish lists of 'quality' builders, you can be sure the lists would be quite short and those on it would have more work than they ever could hope to handle.

Finding a builder

There are no guaranteed methods of success for finding a perfect builder to carry out your work. Good builders themselves are continually trying to locate good tradesmen who they can sub-contract in, and in some trades they are becoming particularly scarce – plasterers and plumbers, to name two. With many alterations, what you really need is a good small builder who works with one or two other people on a regular basis, and who, between them, can accomplish most trades satisfactorily. Kitchen-fitting companies have been working this way for some time, with a just a few electricians, plumbers and gas fitters on hand to alter the services as and when the fitters require.

The market may be vast for such people, but the industry is making it hard for them to exist now because of the growing cost of certification training and accreditation. The registration fees and licensing costs of trading as a gas fitter, for example, have meant that there are few all-round plumbers now who are able to fit WCs and install gas boilers. Instead we have an industry of specialist plumbers who either work on wet plumbing or gas. Indeed, given the latest technical advances in heating and hot water, they have now broken that down further to drainage side plumbing and heating/hot-water plumbing. Oil appliances have also become a specialised field like gas, with their own accreditation body, although in 2004 membership of them is still on a voluntary, not a mandatory basis. Electrical work is heading the same way. The age of specialism is upon us.

All this means that you should be looking at what trades your alterations will involve, and deciding whether to opt for a small general builder, or looking to separate them and employ recognised tradesmen in each field. The latter may work out more cost-effective and to a higher standard, but will undoubtedly test your organisational skills and time.

With structural alterations, general building comes into its own. Basic bricklaying skills are needed for forming piers and building in beams, together with enough knowledge to install enough proper temporary support and proceed carefully, finishing the job with some acceptable plastering. Doesn't sound like much to ask for, does it? And

THE TRADES OF ALTERATION AND REPAIRS

- Roofer
- Bricklayer/general builder
- Carpenter/joiner
- Electrician
- Plasterer
- Plumber
- Gas fitter
- Oil fitter
- Painter and decorator

yet there are plenty of trading 'general builders' who are wholly incapable of achieving this, and some who could go home at night leaving your home partially unsupported. There are some essential checks that you can do to ensure you are employing a professional builder and not one of the others.

Reputation

Good reputations are not hard to hide, bad ones are.

Request a short list of the builder's previous contracts undertaken in the recent past (within the last five years), and once you have received it, speak to their customers and obtain some references. Don't leave it at that, though; for all you know, these people may be relatives or friends of the builder, rather than impartial customers. You could also ask to see their work and visit one of their current or past jobs. You can gain a valuable insight into a general contractor's work, even without possessing building knowledge, by seeing how tidy the work is kept, whether materials are neatly stored and protected or littered around, and whether the home is protected with finishings like stairs, floors and kitchen worktops covered from damage.

You can also enquire with your local authority. The contractor may be on a shortlist of those used for working on council property. Increasingly, councils use outside contractors now, but have thorough vetting procedures for choosing which ones. Building Control Officers have the best idea of who the rogues are and who the good builders are, and they may be willing to give you a few names and numbers, at random of course, without any prejudice, of those you could safely employ.

Insurance

If you are employing one general contractor to do all the work, they should have adequate insurance and you should, before appointing them, ask to see their current certificate of cover. The contractor's Public Liability insurance will protect you from action under civil law should a person be injured by the work. This is not as unlikely as you might think – sales reps, inspectors and others could be visiting your home during the project, and you both have a responsibility towards their safety. If the work fronts onto the road or borders land on other sides, there is a danger of things falling off scaffolds and so on.

There is also the risk of accidental property damage to your home or a neighbouring building, caused directly or indirectly by the work. A broken window, damaged roof or knocked-down fence is one thing on your own property, but damage like this can all too often occur to adjoining properties, and third-party insurance cover is also intended for instances like this.

Builders need Public Liability insurance. Designers benefit from having it, but builders definitely shouldn't trade without it. Check to make sure yours do. A builder can be vicariously liable for the actions of his workmen should they cause accidental damage in your home or injury. As the client, you may choose, however, to sue both the builder and his negligent worker if you suffered at the worker's hands, although court judgements are usually held against the employer, the builder. This is because the builder, with Public Liability insurance, is the person most likely to be able to pay up.

Financial status

With a general contractor you can ask for a banker's reference to establish his financial health. Avoid contractors who request a deposit for materials or whatever up front: those that need it are unlikely to have the financial security necessary to carry out major alterations or repairs, and may already be refused credit at local builders' merchants.

Accreditation checks

Check to see if your builders advertise any trade association membership or the Quality Mark registration. Check the validity of that membership with the association or register holders. Do the builders offer any warranties to cover their work, and at what cost? Are they able to self-certify their work under the Approved Contractor Person Scheme?

Trade federations

Contractors sometimes belong to trade federations and advertise the fact as a symbol of their professionalism or quality of work. You need to understand that all such groups primarily exist to represent the interest of their members, the tradesmen. They are funded by the annual subscriptions of their members, and there are as many different organisations for contractors to join as there are for designers.

Fake membership has been a problem too. One report released in 1996 suggested that between 13 and 22 per cent of all building firms made false declarations about membership of trade associations. Even if you check and find a bona fide member, in practice very little can be interpreted from the fact. The trade bodies representing service trades like plumbing and electrics, for example, are evolving into self-certification. Their members can achieve the right to self-certify their work, and in doing so take responsibility for its compliance with the relevant standards.

The trade federations for general builders always have, and probably (for as long as they survive) always will suffer a bad reputation with the public. The problem is obvious – qualifications are not needed to be a general builder. You could be a fishmonger one day and a trade 'registered' general builder the next. No system of monitoring the work of their members has ever existed, and nobody ever contacts their clients in person to enquire about their customer service. In short, pretty much anybody has been able to join. Some of the country's mass home-builders work in a similar way, employing anybody on building sites when qualified and experienced tradesmen are hard to find. So long as they aren't completely disastrous in what they do, they are usually good enough to be employed.

It's always been that way and it will take a lot to change it, but I am confident that there will be less and less opportunities for cowboy builders in the future. The Approved Contractor Person Schemes that now exist for some trades like gas fitters and electricians could be extended to plasters and roofers in time. Eventually most of the trades could be covered by only qualified and professional tradesmen, registered with recognised bodies. Those general contractors who employ anybody they can get away with paying little to, would find it difficult to exist in such a climate. Of course it would take time and we would all have to get used to checking the IDs of people working on our home, but it would solve an old problem.

Quality Mark scheme

Still in its infancy, if not post-natal care stage (in Spring 2003 only 360 builders were listed on its national register), this scheme may one day evolve into a useful and recognised way of finding professional builders. It is targeted at the home alterations and repairs market, where a proliferation of cowboys has operated for a long time; if nothing else, employing a builder from this register should avoid them. The scheme has been instigated by the Department of Trade and Industry as a Government Initiative, and you can find details in the Contacts pages at the back of this book.

Self-certification (Approved Contractor Person)

Self-certification is the new method of control for some trades and elements of construction. Electrics, oil, gas and heating services, for example, all should come with certificates of installation and testing when they are installed by recognised contractors, to indicate that

they are taking responsibility for the quality of their work.

These individuals should be registered with designated bodies and identified as such. ID cards are carried, and registration is done on an individual, not a company, basis. Here are the trades and the alteration work they can do, together with the designated registration body for each. The details for each are included within the Contacts pages at the back of this book. Remember that out of all these, only gas has mandatory registration – all others are voluntary.

Quotes

You should invite any builder or tradesman to give you a detailed and written quotation for the work (rather than an estimate). A schedule of works should be attached, which should set out the specification in general terms but also state whether plant hire and materials are included. The builders should refer to any drawings and structural calculations that you have in their quotation. In short, look for the detail in the quote and try to spot any differences between what you are asking for and what you are being quoted for.

Estimates

An estimate is exactly that – a best guess. It allows the contractor to present a higher or lower final bill. The figure quoted is not legally binding unless it is supplemented with a written agreement stating that the price shown is a firm price, which effectively converts it to a quotation. Contractors

45

GAS

Installing a gas boiler or fire

CORGI-registered gas fitters approved under the Gas Safety (Installation and Use) Regulations 1988.

OIL

Installing an oil-fired Boiler up to 45kW rated output in a building up to three storeys*

Installing an oil storage tank and supply pipes

OFTEC-registered individuals possessing the relevant certificate for the type of work

---

PLUMBING

Installing above or below ground foul or surface water drainage systems

Installing stored hot water vessels in buildings up to three storeys and where connected to shallow access drainage systems no more than 750 mm deep

Registered individual under the Approved Contractor Person Scheme with the IOP (Institute of Plumbing)

WINDOWS AND DOORS

Replacing a rooflight, roof window, door or window

A person registered under FENSA (Fenestration Self-Assessment Scheme) in respect of that type of work

---

ELECTRICS

Proposed in 2004 – a person registered with the NIEC or the ECA

Alteration work to, or extension of electrical power and lighting circuits

---

* NOTE

The reference to buildings up to three storeys does not include the basement of homes, but denotes any home with more than three storeys above ground.

favour estimates, and many will actively avoid quoting for any work. If this is the case with yours, then try to agree with them in writing a 'maximum price' which will not be exceeded.

Contingency sums

Most building work should have a contingency sum agreed in it, and this should be included with the estimate or quote. The sum can be set by you as the client, or agreed with the contractor. It will only be used to pay for unexpected extras should they occur, and only then in agreement between both parties. In this way, nasty surprises can be catered for but care should be taken to ensure that the sum is only used for work that was unforeseen when the job was priced. If come the end of the job, it was not required, then it will be deducted from the final bill. Typically, a figure representing 3–5 per cent of the estimate or quote would make a contingency sum for most work.

Limited companies

In limited liability companies the individual tradesmen are employees, and as such they hold no personal liability for any breaches of contract or of negligence by the company employing them.

My building law studies were undertaken a long time ago and I tried to sleep through most of them, but I recall this has something to do with the law of agency, an agent in this case being the employee acting on behalf of the employer, known as the principal. The principal gets to carry the can when things go wrong. If you employ a limited company you have no redress against personal individuals; the director of a limited company has duties and responsibilities that are described under the Companies Act.

Daywork

If you cannot agree upon an exact amount for the project because it is unquantifiable by its nature, such as the removal of dry rot, for example, then you might have to agree to daywork with your contractor.

In spite of its name, daywork is normally priced by the man/hour, and you must be careful to monitor the time spent on the work. The best way to achieve this is by maintaining a daywork sheet that you and your contractor can jointly fill in and sign at the end of each day, allowing you both to keep a check on it. The hourly rate should be agreed before work starts, of course. If you aren't providing the plant and materials, the cost of these can be added on or built into the rates, along with your contractor's reasonable overheads and profit.

Written agreements

The simplest forms of contract are written agreements, not verbal agreements – the latter are acts of faith, which are entirely different. With the majority of alteration and repair work being relatively low-cost, it is, however, tempting to settle for something less than a contract.

Full contracts are highly detailed, wordy and lengthy, and appear inappropriate for minor work. They also have an image of legal unpleasantness

Example Invitation to Tender/Letter of Agreement

<name and address of contractor>

Dear............

Ref: ....*<title description of job>*

You are invited to submit a firm quotation for the above.

The work comprises
the..
....and shall include for
incidental works necessary to complete the work to my reasonable satisfaction.

Although a formal contract will not be entered into, the JCT Agreement for Minor
Building Works 1980 Edition (revised 1991 and inclusive of all amendments to date) will
be deemed to apply in the event of any dispute.

Damages for non-completion; liquidated damages will be at the rate of £........ per
day/per week during which the works remain uncompleted.

An amount equal to 2.5% of the total value of the work will be retained for a period
of.........weeks/months after the date of practical completion.

Where applicable, all work is to comply with BS: 8000, Codes of Practice and other
British Standards, material manufacturers recommendations and instructions appropriate
to achieve a satisfactory performance.

The Contractor is to inspect the site of the work prior to submission of the quotation.
No subsequent claim arising from failure to do so will be entertained. All costs incurred
in preparing the tender shall be borne by the contractor.

Include in your quotation the provisional Sum of .... For contingent or unforeseen
works as identified in the schedule of works.

This sum to be deducted in whole or part as agreed by both parties if not required.

The works are to commence on ....and be completed
by..................................

The specification shall be fully priced and a pricing summary sheet duly completed,
signed and dated with the company address. The completed quotation should be sent to:

<your name and address>

and must be received not later than.................*<date required>*

Yours faithfully,

....

Enclosed: Schedule of Work

that give an impression of mistrust: not a pleasant way to start business. What is needed is something more simple that is legally binding, and to which you can add detail if you want, by way of a schedule. Letters of Agreement can also be used as Invitations to Tender for work. They usually invoke by condition the full rights of an industry standard contract (a JCT contract in the example shown opposite) should things go awry.

Payments

Stage payments are the usual accepted method of paying for work. Agreed in advance at what stages in the project it will occur, an agreed amount is released when each stage is complete. This is not a system for paying in advance – it is a system for paying in arrears that avoids builders from becoming financially overstretched. It is thus relevant to large or timely projects, such as underpinning, but not minor alterations, such as installing a new window.

Paying by credit

The safest method of payment is by credit card, which affords you some protection under the Credit Protection Act. If you have fallen into the trap of paying a deposit to a contractor who then goes out of business before starting the work, this act should allow you to recover the payment. If the contractor doesn't have a credit card scheme, then you might ask for a deposit indemnity. In the case of a limited company, its directors should be able to provide this, and if it isn't limited, the proprietor should. Of course, you must remember that the

indemnities will only work if you can locate these people personally – and they have a habit if disappearing if the firm has gone bust!

If you are paying by credit, whether it be by card or by loan, including those loans in which the contractor is acting as the broker, as some package firms do, you have rights under the Consumer Credit Act 1974.

Warranties

One worthwhile benefit of choosing a trade-registered or Quality Mark contractor is the option to buy a warranty on their work. Cover is normally for a period of up to ten years from the date of completion – against financial loss arising from any defects with inferior workmanship or materials, and against the event of the contractor becoming insolvent, or dying, before finishing the work. The drawback is that in the first instance, claims usually have to be against failures that occur in the first two years. With these policies, you can expect that if you seriously fall out with your contractor in the middle of the job, a refereeing service will be provided to arbitrate between you and, if necessary, an alternative contractor appointed to finish the job. This would also apply if the contractor went bankrupt, died or simply disappeared before finishing the work.

Warranties are insurance policies like any other. You pay a fee that is often somewhere between 1 and 2 per cent of the contract sum, and you are covered for ten years or so against particular misadventures.

You can also expect to be protected

against the loss of a deposit paid to the contractor. Structural failures are normally covered for the full period of the warranty, since they are more unlikely to occur. Make sure that the cover extends to sub-contractors or nominated suppliers engaged in the project by your contractor. Not many contractors complete work these days without using some sub-contracted labour somewhere along the way.

Normally, any insurance warranty covers the property, and if you sell up before the term ends, the cover automatically passes to the new owners of the home.

Although the cost of all this insurance will not be insignificant, it is the price you pay for peace of mind in a building industry fraught with problems of disputes and poor workmanship. In time, perhaps, the 'free insurance' currently enjoyed with some materials will be extended to all qualified tradesmen and their work.

DIY

DIY repairs

Being capable of maintaining your own home with basic repairs can be a definite asset, saving you a good deal of trouble and expense. Without some understanding of what needs doing and how to do it, DIY can also cost you a good deal of trouble and expense.

Second to not having sufficient knowledge, what makes DIY difficult is not having the right tools. You can struggle for ages with an adjustable spanner to release a bath tap, but armed with a tap spanner that is not only sized specifically for taps but has right-angled

open ends to get at the nut from underneath, the job takes a few minutes. There are specialised tools for so many jobs, and owning all of them is going to be uneconomical, but some are indispensable. Take wire strippers, for example: electrical work isn't physically difficult, but making do with a knife to strip the insulation off cables is twice as awkward and dangerous. You can so easily nick the insulation off the inner wires, exposing the copper and risking it shorting out, using a knife. That won't happen with wire strippers, which are gauged to strip the outer sheaf of insulation effortlessly and cleanly.

Power tools are becoming cheaper and more diverse, but some are suited only to light use. I have lost count of the number of cheap electric grinders that I've seen burned out after only a short life – cheap tools are fine if you know that they have limitations. A 9-volt cordless drill will bore holes in softwood without effort, but it won't have much effect on masonry walls. For that you would need an 18-volt cordless with hammer action, if not a mains-powered drill. Their power output in watts will give you an indication of what they can do, but it's worth noting the difference in quality between tools aimed at the DIY market and those at the professional market. If you want tools to last, buying quality will pay off in the end.

DIY replacement

It may seem like a moot point, but with every repair that you do, take a moment to consider replacing it rather than fixing it. There are plenty of times when it will be more economical and easier to do the former. Let me give you an example of what I mean: I recently spent half a day trying to fix a dripping garden tap. Having bought a pack of tap washers, I found that they weren't sitting flat enough to stop the leak. Off I went to buy a re-seating tool, which was clearly aimed at the DIY market and proved hopelessly inadequate for grinding down the brass seating sufficient for my new washers. I finally noticed that to replace the faulty tap with a new one was the same amount that I'd already spent. It took a couple of minutes to unscrew and replace the old one.

It goes against the grain, but repairing these days often means replacing. Those kitchen ceramic block mixer taps might not have washers to leak; instead they leak from the neck of the pillar. Yes there is a tiny brass screw on the back to release them, but kitchen sinks and their taps usually go up against kitchen walls, and you won't stand a chance of getting a screwdriver between them.

Improved repair

Having decided whether to replace or repair, consider whether you can do anything to improve on what has failed – not only to prevent it failing again, but also to improve on your home and its services. An example would be when replacing a broken window hinge: if you have a standard scissor-type hinge (common to UPVC windows), you could replace it with one incorporating a child-safety catch or a means-of-escape hinge that opens fully out.

In Feng Shui terms it is said to be bad (Sha) Chi to have water flowing directly towards your home, but even worse Chi to have it flowing directly through it, which must make a burst water pipe one of life's most unsettling events. It can be repaired with a simple straight piece of copper tube and compression fitting at each end; or if it's close to an appliance you could take the opportunity to fit a chrome in-line valve. These flush-fit valves take only a quarter turn with a screwdriver to operate, and close off the water supply for maintenance to a tap or appliance. The cost is negligible and the benefits are enormous – you won't have to turn off the supply at the stopcock and deprive the entire home of water when you next want to fit new taps.

The priority with any burst water pipe is to turn off the supply and locate the leak. Copper tubing in floors is easily damaged by the nailing of boards, and it helps to know where your pipes run. To make sure your repair section doesn't leak at the joints, cut the pipe cleanly and straight, use a little PTFE tape over the thread, and don't overtighten the compression joints. It is possible to crack the olives by being overenthusiastic with the spanners – they need to be tight, but not that tight.

My first burst water pipe served a good part of the town and was found by a piling rig while I was covering for a site agent on holiday. I like to imagine that the waterspout, which erupted for several hours and rivalled the one in Lake Geneva, compensated for the loss of water to so many homes by entertaining small children for miles.

DIY safety

Where did the phrase as 'safe as houses' come from? We are constantly being reminded that our homes are accident blackspots. 2,500,000 people need medical treatment every year after accidentally injuring themselves in their own home, and on average ten people a day are beyond medical treatment. About 10 per cent of these figures are DIY-related, of which hundreds involve power tools. Not a pleasant thought, but given the popularity of DIY and the ever-increasing range of cheap power tools available, these figures can only rise.

Men in their thirties are the group most likely to be represented in these statistics, presumably because they are the ones most likely to be doing DIY in the first place, although clearly the risks are open to everyone.

Staying safe while you work is really about planning what you're going to do, working in enough space and using common sense - it also really helps if you've left yourself enough time to do the job. Don't start work on the plumbing system an hour before everyone is due home, pushing you to get the water supply back on.

If it helps, remember that DIY is meant to take that bit longer than getting a professional in (and tell your partner I said so) - one, you are working on your own home and have a lot of respect for it; two, you're having to think about what you're doing the whole time; and three, you're not practised at it. The good thing is that if you remember all these things, it will help you to stay safe.

As for statistics? Well apparently, several hundred people hospitalise themselves each year by stepping into or setting fire to their pyjamas - which can't be easy, can it?

CHAPTER 4

Structural Alterations

Forming openings in loadbearing walls

Forgive me for rewinding the tape a bit, but to begin with we really need to consider when a wall is loadbearing and when it isn't. Later on, when you're ready to share this knowledge with people at bus stops, it might help you to think of the 'When is a door not a door…' riddle and transcribe it to the 'When is a wall not a wall?' version – 'When it's a partition.' In this way you can safely think of any wall as loadbearing and any wall that isn't as a partition – although by this time the bus may have turned up.

Walls are thought of as loadbearing when they carry load (or weight) from some other part of the building. With internal walls it's a common mistake to interpret loadbearing as meaning only floor loads, when in truth roof or ceiling loads can bear on them, or indeed other walls. The upstairs walls in a house can sometimes be supported on beams or doubled-up joists, which are in turn supported by inner walls, but these may carry weight from the roof by way of struts supporting purlins in the attic. Ceiling joists in traditional roofs are often supported on inner walls and when they are, they are usually topped by a timber wall plate for the joist to sit on. If this isn't enough, inner walls might also act as loadbearing elements by buttressing the outer walls and offering them support against the effects of wind-loading.

Only by exploring the construction of your home will you know for sure which are the loadbearing walls and which are not. The Preliminaries chapter of this book will help guide you in surveying your home and sketching up a plan of the loadbearing elements, but a structural engineer should carry out a detailed survey as part of the overall design.

If your aim is to convert two rooms into one by removing a wall entirely, knowing what load it carries, if any, is critical. It will decide on the nature of the beam and the minimum size necessary to replace it, and indeed whether any piers should be retained at the end bearings of the beam. Even if the latter aren't, padstones are likely to be needed at the bearings, and these should be designed, too.

A structural engineer can calculate the load imposed from each element of construction, total them up and determine the ultimate design load for the beam. Armed with this figure (expressed in kilograms), the beam itself can be specified. It may be timber or steel or a combination of the two, known as a flitch beam. It is worth asking your engineer to resolve a choice of beams for you; two or three will give you some latitude for pricing and purchasing later.

Proceeding in safety

You can think of buildings being built from elements; like blocks in the game of Jenko, you can safely remove some elements but not others. To change a wall or part of a wall for a beam, some way of temporarily supporting the

53

structure is needed while the change takes place. Without it, the building can collapse.

It follows that the 'temporary support' itself must be strong enough and correctly placed before the wall can be taken down or the opening formed in it. A wall that is supporting a floor or a ceiling can be relieved of this load by installing a row of adjustable steel props

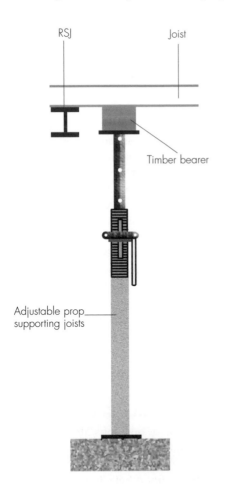

Temporary support in place.

to a bearing plate (usually 100 x 100 mm PAR) under the ceiling. As items of plant, props can be hired, but most builders will have purchased their own for frequent use. These props have a load capacity in themselves, and proper temporary support sometimes needs to be calculated and planned along with the beam installation itself. Where it isn't designed, it is best to be overcautious and put in more than you need (perhaps less than 1 m apart).

Inside your home you will want to protect your finishings from the props themselves, and clean timber bearers should be used in any case, to distribute the load. A typical floor support may have props spaced at 2 m intervals beneath a bearing timber running parallel with the wall to be demolished.

If the wall continues up through the floor above (or if you are supporting a chimney stack), temporary support can only be provided by pinning the remaining structure with needles, short beams that run though the wall at right angles and are supported either side of it by adjustable props. They aren't always necessary, because brickwork does have some ability to arch over gaps – but only when it is in good condition. Even then, it is only worth relying on across small openings and where point loads don't occur above.

The arching effect is sometimes used in structural design to calculate a reduced load above an opening where only a continuous wall bears over it. It takes a triangle area of load, rather than the total area of the wall, and uses this to resolve the beam or lintel.

The idea with props is that they

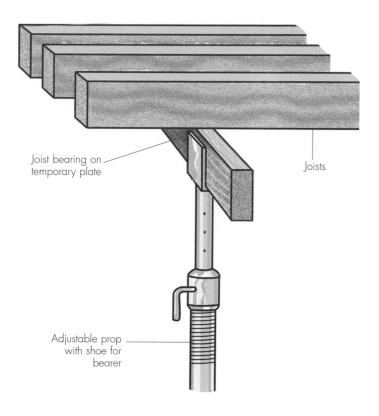

Joist bearing on
temporary plate

Joists

Adjustable prop
with shoe for
bearer

Props can be used to support bearers and needle beams.

should accept the weight from the floor above, not try to jack it up. Overenthusiastic propping is a common mistake, and one that often results in damaged homes, with cracks appearing in other parts of the house.

By overtightening props the joists can be accidentally lifted and any partition walls supported on them shifted. With scenarios like this, a crack can occur some distance from where the beam is installed and builders may claim that it can't be related to their

work. It makes sense to take your builder on a guided tour of your home, to discuss which parts are to be supported by the new beam and also to jointly note the condition of the walls before work starts. This could save a lot of debate later on.

Internal walls should always be demolished by hand and with care. An alternative way would be to use a disc cutter, but you'd be hoovering up the dust for months afterwards. Dust sheets aren't going to help, unless you thought

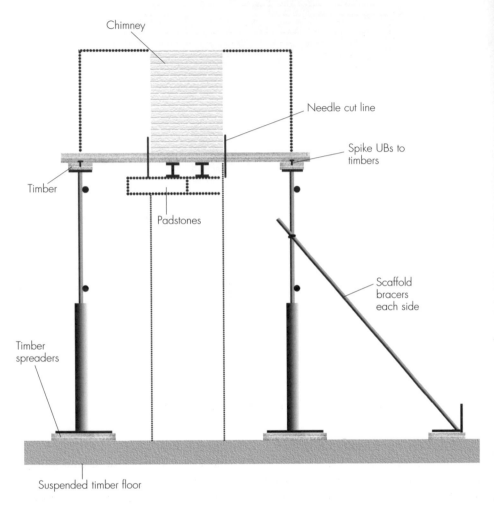

Chimney

Needle cut line

Spike UBs to timbers

Timber

Padstones

Scaffold bracers each side

Timber spreaders

Suspended timber floor

Temporary support to chimney removals should be designed.

you were going to cover the walls and ceilings with them to and tape up the gaps around the doors. Disc cutters are not indoor tools; they require total ventilation of the kind that you can only get outdoors and a light breeze prevailing away from you and any open windows. The quantity of dust they generate is extraordinary, and the speed of cutting the opening is only negated by the time spent clearing up. With internal wall removal, what you need is hand tools: lump hammers and club hammers and bolsters or cold chisels. Blockwork walls can be taken down very easily with block saws equipped with large teeth. In fact, with a hole drilled through a blockwork wall and the opening marked out in chalk, an opening can quickly be cut out by hand sawing and hammering.

It must go without saying that builders are not always the most tenacious of people, and to be fair to them, knocking down walls and installing beams isn't needlework, but it makes sense to remove furniture and valued possessions from the area – if not the room. I left a site once to the sound of a prop falling over into an antique glass display cabinet.

End bearings

For beams of any material to work effectively, they need to be supported by adequate end bearings. The bearing is often as much a part of the design as the beam itself. To put it simply, in a beam with one point of bearing at each end and no other means of support, all of the load plus the weight of the beam itself is divided between the bearings equally, and focused into a small area at that. In most cases this means that padstones of some description should be built in for the beam to sit on, and these serve to spread the load out into the wall or pier on which they in turn sit. The size and nature of the padstones depend on two things: the strength of the wall or pier beneath it, and the load from the beam. These factors are used to calculate the area of the padstone. Most commonly concrete is employed

although sometimes two courses of engineering bricks will be used.

Engineering bricks

Engineering bricks are hard, the SAS of the brick world, with unit strengths as high as 69 n/sq mm in compression, and so they can resist point loads without cracking or crushing. They also have the advantage of being quick and easy to bed in place while the beam is still supported by props. Concrete padstones are a pain if cast in situ, since a box of shuttering (like a mould) has to be made around the pier on which the concrete can be set. It should be left for at least seven days to cure before the beam is dry-packed to it and able to be supported by it. The full strength of concrete will not be achieved for 28 days. You don't have this delay with engineering bricks, but if you are faced with a concrete padstone design it is worth checking to see if a precast concrete option can be used.

Lintels

Some companies manufacture padstones in a few standard sizes, but precast lintels are an alternative. Lintels have a compressive strength of around 50 n/mm sq and are available in a variety of widths and lengths; if necessary, they can be cut with a disc cutter to the size required for the padstone. Where they are particularly useful is in cavity walls or 100 mm wide walls where piers aren't wanted to support the beam. In this situation, a beam over an internal cross wall can span right across the full width to the external walls to create a clear opening.

The precast concrete padstones can be used in their manufactured lengths as spreaders to distribute the load along the length of the wall. This of course needs to be checked by an engineer, as often the inner leaf of a cavity wall is built of soft insulation blocks with very low compressive strengths – not ideal for beam bearings, but if circumstances allow, a long spreader lintel can be a popular solution. When piers are needed, they can be cut and retained from the original wall, or rebuilt from the foundations up.

Other piers

Concrete blocks are a fast and usually cheap way of building piers, but their quality and strength can vary enormously, so check with your builder's merchants what they have available – some may be as low as 7 n/sq mm, and others as high as 20 n/sq mm. Most of us would want to see blockwork piers plastered and decorated, but some blocks are clean and smooth-finished enough to be left exposed; the term for any exposed masonry in the industry is 'fair-faced'. I can see this working if you're after the industrial interior-design look that says 'factory' when you walk into the lounge, but otherwise, bricks are likely to be the answer.

Stock bricks are the popular choice for 'fair-face' piers, or at least they are when exposed brickwork is in fashion – and old handmade stock bricks at that. In the 1980s we went through a period of wanting to make our walls look rustic and partially dilapidated. A lot of family pubs were being built in this style, with old farming tools hanging off the walls, and I think it rubbed off on some of us. It works well in old cottages and conversions, but it often means that the core of the pier has to be built out of engineering bricks for structural stability and the 'olde worlde' stock bricks are used only as superficial cladding around the outside. You will end up with an oversized pier, but it will be an 'olde worlde' oversized pier that you can nail a scythe to, if that's what you want.

With timber beams, timber posts can sometimes be used in lieu of piers, but they do require connections that restrain the beam, which traditionally would include knee braces to stiffen the joint. Knee braces are the curved timbers that have been cut from the bow joint of the tree and are then tenon-jointed into the posts and beams of barns.

Packing beams

With the padstones and piers in place, all that remains is to see that the beam is dry-packed to the underside with the padstone. Pieces of slate were traditionally used for this job, but it can be done with the modern equivalent or cement and sharp sand dry mortar, the aim here being to make sure the beam is fully supported through its bearing before the temporary support is removed from its position.

Stiffening beams

I know how difficult it is to imagine, having just seen two tonnes of RSJ heaved into your lounge, but steel beams often need to be restrained. It is easy to see why most of us think the only way they can go is down, but restraining them laterally is often necessary. If your RSJ is supporting a floor, then it is easy to either run the joists into the web of the beam or mechanically fix them to the top, and this will restrain it beautifully.

An example of a beam that is unrestrained is where it supports only a wall above and no fixing is possible between it and the wall. In this instance the beam can distort laterally, with nothing to hold it in place. This isn't a problem if the engineer has designed it under this condition, because it will have been allowed for in resolving the beam. An RSJ with the compression flange (top flange) fully restrained along its length can span further that one of the same size that is in an unrestrained condition.

Timber stud walls will have a sole plate at the bottom under which the beam can be placed, hence it is possible to drill the compression flange for

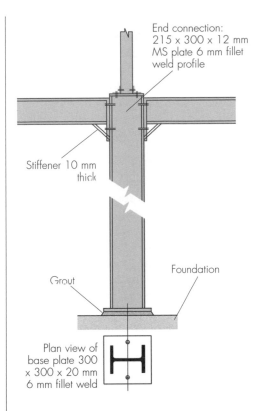

End connection: 215 x 300 x 12 mm MS plate 6 mm fillet weld profile

Stiffener 10 mm thick

Foundation

Grout

Plan view of base plate 300 x 300 x 20 mm 6 mm fillet weld

Steel beams supported by a steel column.

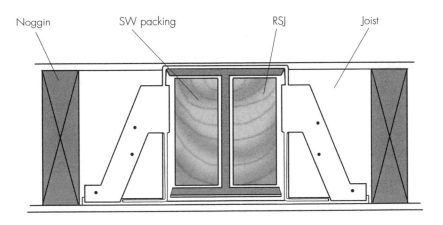

Noggin   SW packing   RSJ   Joist

Floor beam RSJ with joists supported on strap-over-type hangars.

coach screws up into the plate. Likewise, floor joists can be spiked to a plate that is mechanically fixed to the RSJ before it is lifted into position. Fixing is much easier then by bolting or shot-firing the plate down. Whatever you choose for your fixings, they should not exceed 600 mm centres.

Timber beams

Timber strength varies from species to species and within species, so to help designers specify timber strength classes have been formed, which group together timber of a known and graded maximum strength. They were numbered 1 to 10 once with a SC (strength class) prefix, but that must have been too easy for people to understand because it didn't last long and a more obscure method has since been adopted. The SC has been replaced by C, and the standard grade whitewood used as structural timber is now known as C16, previously SC3 and previous to that GS grade. The permitted stress of C16, measured perpendicular to the grain (as a beam would be in bending), is accepted as 5.3 n/mm sq. C24 (previously SC4 and SS grade) has a tighter grain and is hence stronger, achieving 7.5 n/mm sq.

Timber beams are chosen for one or more of three reasons: ease, economy or appearance. Ease can be a bit of a red herring if you're simply thinking timber will be lighter to handle than steel. Hardwoods like oak are incredibly heavy in large beams, and the required section in an RSJ is likely to be lighter. Ease really comes into the equation with fixings, if you have joists to

---

CHOOSING TIMBER FROM A SALVAGE YARD – A CHECKLIST

- The length of timber you need, including the end bearings. Structural designers will have quoted an effective span in their calculations, which is less than the actual length, so use a tape measure across the room and not the designer's calculations.

- Timber that is relatively straight in the horizontal plane so that it aligns well with the supported wall or floor.

- Avoid damp or rotted beams, which may have been dragged from a farm pond or been exposed to damp for too long. You don't want to introduce wet rot into your home, or a weak beam.

---

support or a cladding to be fixed around the beam.

Economy is fine when the load allows it, and it goes without saying that a timber beam will carry less weight than a steel one of the same size. Timber, however, is sure to be cheaper pound for pound.

Appearance is more often sought in old cottages, for example, where a degree of exposed wood already exists. Oak is the favourite choice, not only because it is strong but also because it is aesthetic and adds character to your home. It was used to form the entire structural frame of a house as far back as the 13th century, when oak was in plentiful supply, and so you can also hang your hat on it being a traditional material for home use.

We seem to have traded our native woodlands and forests for roads and estates since the thirteenth century, and new oak is now often imported from France and other countries, where the supply is greater and hence cheaper. In any event it is well-seasoned oak that you should look for, and a salvage yard of secondhand materials is the place to find it. Green (new) oak has a high moisture content that will go through a

TYPICAL CHARRING RATES OF TIMBER	
Softwood	15 mm per 30 minutes
Oak and teak	9 mm per 30 minutes

painful drying-out process in a centrally heated home, causing it to split and twist. With seasoned oak, so long as it has been kept in the dry, this won't be a problem.

Fire resistance of timber beams

As if this book isn't already packed full of unexpected facts, here comes another one: timber beams can be chosen for fire resistance. Wood, given enough of it, has a measurable performance in a fire that can be used to justify it without any fire-resisting cladding. This is because it chars at a given rate of so many millimetres per minute, depending on the species.

If your beam needs to still be there safely doing its job after 30 minutes for example, having a half-hour fire resistance, it could be overdesigned to illustrate that after 30 minutes worth of charring the residual section is structurally big enough to carry the load. An engineer might reverse-design this by designing an oak beam and then adding on the charring rate dimensions to the result and specifying the oversized beam as the minimum section dimensions you need to buy.

Of course, if three sides of the beam are exposed, it has to be assumed that the charring will occur simultaneously in a fire and so the total loss of section

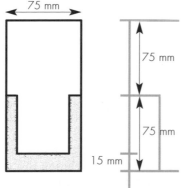

A section through a partly exposed timber beam, showing sacrificial area.

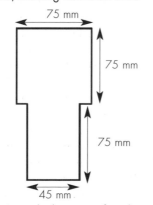

The beam's residual section after charring.

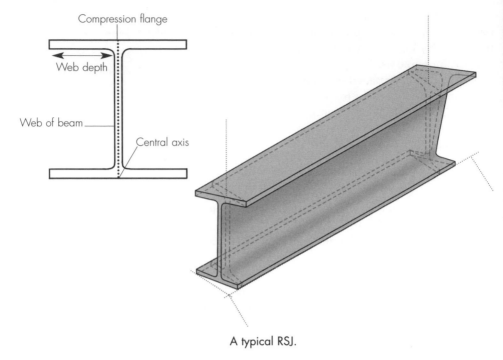

Compression flange

Web depth

Web of beam

Central axis

A typical RSJ.

can be quite significant. This method works best with oak beams, which have a low charring rate and are often used in big chunky sections for aesthetic effect anyway.

RSJ beams

The acronym RSJ (rolled steel joist) is used commonly to describe a steel beam in the same way that breeze blocks are used to describe all building blocks. In fact, RSJs are limited to steel beams of a certain size and manufacturing process and RSCs, UBs and UCs are more prolific. It matters not what the shape of the beam and its size is, so long as it has been design-checked to carry the load and it fits your needs.

Steel beams have been fabricated in this country since the late 19th century,

replacing cast iron, which had made its debut in the late 1700s, steel being a mixture of iron and carbon that can be rolled hot into shaped beams that can be bolted or welded together. The original I-shaped beams are the ones referred as RSJs, although today fewer sections are made in this form and the range of sizes is limited and more lightweight than other types.

UBs, or universal beams, are typically heavier and able to carry much greater loads. In their symmetrical forms, commonly used as columns, or posts if you prefer, they are known as UCs (universal columns). 203 x 203 mm UCs make ideal beams to support solid, one-brick-thick walls across considerable spans, and are often used in the course of domestic alterations.

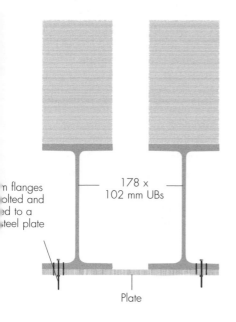

n flanges
olted and
ed to a
steel plate

178 x
102 mm UBs

Plate

Two RSJs supporting a cavity wall.

Steel is priced by weight, and all steel beams are specified by size and weight, with most sizes having a variety of thicknesses (gauges) and varying weights expressed in kilos per metre. Weight is often considered to be a drawback for the use of steel at high level, since having to haul the material into position is a major part of the job. Ground-floor openings, however, are ideal for steel beams particularly where masonry walls have to be supported. Steel isn't going to shrink or split like timber, and with good bearings you know once it's in, it will last forever.

Given an I-shaped section, joists can be supported within the web of the beam on the bottom flange to lose the beam inside the structure, or more

RSCs (channel sections) are also available from quite small sizes through to larger, half-column, dimensions. One of the great advantages of steel beams is that they don't deteriorate much and have great secondhand use. Because of this, steel beams can be picked up from salvage and scrap yards, the only difficulty being that they are likely to be of discontinued sizes, if not actually of imperial dimensions; they are not present in the structural steel tables used today, making it harder to assess the structural properties and safe bearing capacity. Some information on historic steel beam sizes has been published, but if your engineer doesn't have access to them, a comparison with the contemporary equivalents may have to be made.

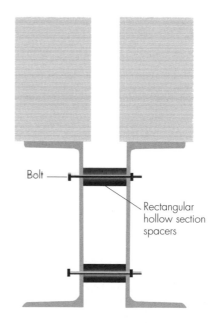

Bolt

Rectangular
hollow section
spacers

Detail showing connection of channels
supporting a cavity wall.

63

STANDARD STEEL BEAM SIZES
UBs
127 x 76 mm (x 13 kg/m)
152 x 89 mm (x 16 kg/m)
178 x 102 mm (x 19 kg/m)
203 x 102 mm (x 23 kg/m)
203 x 133 mm (x 30 kg/m)
UCs
152 x 152 mm (x 30 kg/m)
203 x 203 mm (x 46 kg/m)
203 x 203 mm (x 60 kg/m)
203 x 203 mm (x 86 kg/m)
RSJs
89 x 89 mm (x 19.35 kg/m)
102 x 102 mm (x 23.07 kg/m)
152 x 127 mm (x 37.20 kg/m)
203 x 152 mm (x 52.09 kg/m)
RSCs
127 x 64 mm (x 14.90 kg/m)
152 x 76 mm (x 17.88 kg/m)
152 x 89 mm (x 23.84 kg/m)
178 x 89 mm (x 26.81 kg/m)
203 x 89 mm (x 29.78 kg/m)
229 x 89 mm (x 32.76 kg/m)

NOTE:
The beam sizes and weights quoted above are examples of those that have been commonly used in structural alterations. They represent a selection of what is available from an ever-growing list. Although the beams currently manufactured by the steel industry may not include some of those sizes quoted, they have all at some time been commonly produced. As a large part of the domestic steel beam market is filled by secondhand beams, I have included them here.

commonly on the top compression flange of the beam. It helps if the joists can be mechanically fixed to the beam, restraining it laterally, and this necessitates the use of a timber plate to nail them to. The plate can be bolted down or shot-fired into the steel before it is installed.

As strong as steel is, it does perform badly in a fire. At 550° C (quickly reached in a fire) steel weakens by 30 per cent in tensile strength – enough to cause collapse – and because of this, fire protection has to be added to it. You can do this in the traditional way, by cladding it with plasterboard and plaster finish, or you can paint it with a fire-resistant intumescent paint. Specialised paints come in a variety of colours if you're trying to create that Industrial Conversion look in your home, but they can equally be used when you want to face the beam with a thin cladding of plastic or one of the many timber veneers available.

Secondhand steel beams

Safe load tables for historic beams are still available, and so if you do acquire an old beam, even an imperial one, it is possible for an engineer to determine its suitability.

In the example on page 65, of RSJs manufactured in the early 1960s, I have converted the published safe loads in imperial tons over spans measured in feet to metric. As a rough guide you can convert an old ton to a metric tonne (1000 kg) by multiplying to the factor of 1.016. The resulting value can be multiplied by a thousand to transfer it to kilos, and then into force by

SAFE WORKING LOADS OVER GIVEN SPANS

CLEAR SPAN OF OPENING

Beam size	2.5 m	3 m	3.5 m	4 m
SWL values in kilonewtons				
102 x 102 x 23 kg/m	51	46	42	32
127 x 76 x 16 kg/m	47	39	34	30
152 x 89 x 17 kg/m	61	51	44	38
178 x 102 x 21 kg/m	90	75	64	56
203 x 102 x 25 kg/m	119	99	85	75
203 x 152 x 52 kg/m	249	207	178	156

NOTE:
The safe working loads shown are quoted where the compression (top) flange of the beam is afforded some lateral restraint. Where this is not present (eg where only a wall is supported on the beam without floor loads or intersecting beams), a figure representing 70 per cent of these values should be considered as the maximum.

USEFUL CONVERSION FACTORS

1 ton = 1.016 tonne

Tonne x 9.81 = kilonewton

	SPANS (metres)			
Beam size (weight)	3 m	4 m	5 m	6 m
10 x 4 (19) RSJ	129	108	86	71
8 x 5.25 (17) RSJ	96	80	64	53
10 x 5.75 (25) RSJ	181	151	121	101
inches (weight in pounds per foot)		(safe working loads in kn)		

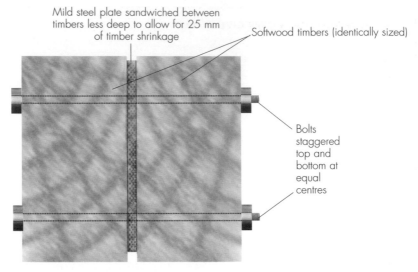

Mild steel plate sandwiched between timbers less deep to allow for 25 mm of timber shrinkage

Softwood timbers (identically sized)

Bolts staggered top and bottom at equal centres

Cross section of a flitch beam.

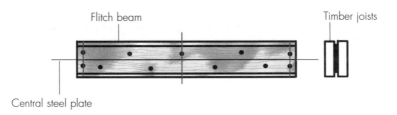

Flitch beam

Timber joists

Central steel plate

Bolting pattern of flitch beam in elevation.

multiplying to 9.81 (the speed of gravity bit), or ten if you prefer to keep life simple, which puts the figure into newtons. To complete the conversion into kilonewtons, simply divide by 1000 because there are a thousand newtons in a kilonewton. For the mathematically gifted I won't have to explain how this formula can be shortened, but for myself and the rest of you, you can just take your metric tonnes and multiply by 9.81 (or 10) and

you have the same answer – the safe working load in kn.

Flitch beams

Halfway between the RSJ and the timber beam lies the flitch beam – a hybrid of the two. It comprises a pair of timbers (joist sizes) and a mild steel plate sandwiched in between and running the full length of the beam. The three elements are held together by bolts at frequent intervals, and these bolted connections cause the beam to act as a single unit, sharing the load between each element, the load each takes being proportional to the stiffness of that element. The depth of the flitch beam plays a large part in how much load it can take, but the thickness of the timbers and, to a greater extent, the steel plate, can also make it stronger.

Flitch beams are typically 150–225 mm deep, comprising two 50-mm wide timbers and a steel plate anywhere from 6 mm to 25 mm thick. Mild steel plate is manufactured in 2-mm thick increments. The bolts holding it together are usually spaced at equal centres, 400–600 mm apart, staggered from top to bottom to prevent a line of splitting occurring. They are normally doubled at the bearings to carry the reaction in the steel plate. Bolts come in a variety of sizes and need to be designed by your engineer as an integral part of the beam, since their size (diameter) and their grade will need to be appropriate to the shear placed on them. Bolts have a shear strength capacity beyond which they can fail. Invariably M16 bolts are used, but sometimes M12s are sufficient. The steel plate is best kept 25 mm shallower in depth than the timbers (eg: 50 x 200 CI6 + 10 x 175 MS plate), since this will accommodate any shrinkage of the timber later as it dries out.

The advantages of flitch beams are obvious. Stronger than timber beams, they provide a potentially cheaper option to a steel RSJ, and they offer timber-to-timber connection. Instead of having to bolt or shot-fire timber plates

to a steel beam before joists or stud walls can be supported from it, you can fix direct to the beam. Not only that, but they are considerably easier to fire-protect, as plasterboard can be screwed directly to them, avoiding the tiresome task of fixing battens that goes with encasing a steel beam.

Adding a new window or door

Creating the wall opening

Openings for windows and doors are often relatively narrow, and the brickwork can be self-supporting temporarily. If there is enough brickwork above an opening, it can do an arching trick which allows it to stay there while you cut the hole out and install the lintel. Clearly there are situations where this doesn't work:

● Where beams arrive over the opening and bear on the wall directly above it

● Where floor joists are supported on the wall directly above it

● Where another opening exists in the wall above it

● Where rafters and ceiling joists are supported on the wall directly above it

● Where the opening is too wide

In all these cases, temporary support should be employed before the opening is cut out. Temporary support can easily be provided to the elements that bear

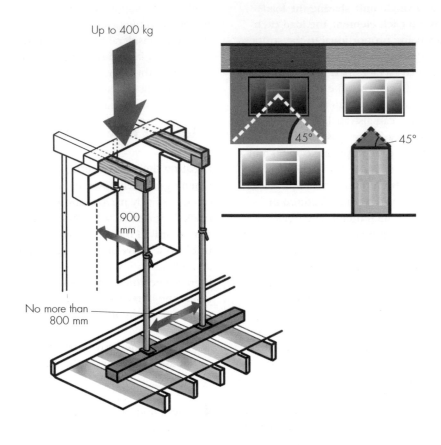

Up to 400 kg

900 mm

No more than 800 mm

45°

45°

Needles shown here can support small loads on suspended floors.

on the wall by using adjustable props aside the opening as near as is practicable to it without actually preventing you from getting at it.

If the opening itself needs to be supported, perhaps because of its width, needles can be used to support the brickwork directly over it. Needles are best described by diagram, but think of them as short lengths of beam that

are threaded through the wall as the opening is cut, and supported either side of the wall by adjustable props, perhaps via a beam run on top of them. Although needles only pick up the weight of the wall in places, they effectively reduced the width of the opening to the centres at which they are placed. In doing so, they ensure that the wall doesn't collapse before the

TYPICAL EXAMPLES OF MANUFACTURED STEEL LINTEL SAFE WORKING LOADS

Box section pressed steel lintel		Standard duty	Heavy duty
100 mm wide x 150 mm high	1.65–2.1 m long	25 kn	30–50 kn
	2.25–2.7 m long	20 kn	30 kn
100 mm wide x 215 mm high	2.7–4.5 m long	30 kn	35–50 kn
	4.8 m long	26 kn	
250 mm cavity wall lintel		Standard duty	Heavy duty
	0.75–1.5 m	15 kn	23–30 kn
	1.65–1.8 m	18 kn	30–35 kn
	1.95–2.1 m	20 kn	41–49 kn
	2.25–2.4 m	22 kn	41–49 kn
	2.55–3.9 m	26 kn	33–54 kn

NOTES:
- The lengths shown are lintel lengths, not span of openings.

- The thickness or gauge of steel lintel varies with the duty and length of lintel, hence the variation with heavy-duty types and the need to assess the loads applied before ordering.

- Where high ranges occur in SWLs it can be assumed that the largest figures are afforded to the shortest lengths in that range.

lintel is installed. For the safest of installations, the needles can be cut and inserted through the wall above the actual position of the lintel, thus allowing the lintel to be inserted before they are individually removed and the holes made good with masonry. In other situations it may be possible to work the lintel into position, removing the needles as you go.

Steel lintels

Manufactured galvanised steel lintels are available for almost every situation imaginable. The larger manufacturers have 50-plus different types in their catalogues, and each type is designed for a particular situation. It is extraordinary to note that in spite of the fact that there is almost certainly a right type of lintel for every job, it is not always the one you see used. Builders are not great at planning ahead and prefer to wait until the day of the job to trundle down to the merchants to buy what they need. What merchants keep in stock, of course, is what is most commonly used – the standard types, not necessarily what they should use. So the problem is self-propelling. It is worth establishing the lintel specification well in advance, because it may need to be ordered and orders can take several weeks.

Where lintels do reach their limits, it is more often a case of supply and economics, rather than structural potential. Special-order extreme heavy-duty lintels are usually forged from RSJ or channel sections and angle irons welded together, and can carry very high loads (up to 90 kn, for example) across openings 4 or 5 m wide. Whether or not you can afford to wait for them to be delivered, or get a price comparable to a regular RSJ arrangement is another matter.

Precast concrete lintels

As with steel lintels, precast concrete lintels are manufactured in standard lengths and sizes, and with allowable loads for each. Concrete lintels are lightly reinforced, but even so, their abilities are much reduced compared to steel lintels. On the plus side, they are relatively cheap and easy to install above openings in masonry walls. The loads and lintel types available to you are variable from one manufacturer to another, but some examples of typical performance are given in the table below as a rough guide.

The table shows the maximum load in kilonewtons (kn) that each lintel at the spans shown will take. It assumes that the loading is evenly distributed along the length of the lintel (as it would be with a wall above, for example), and that the lintels have a least 150 mm of bearing length at each end.

The most popular of these lintel types, and thus the one most commonly available, is the 63 x 100 mm size,

MAXIMUM LOAD IN KILONEWTONS THAT PRECAST CONCRETE LINTELS WILL TAKE AT THESE SPANS								
Size	**Span of opening (not length of lintel)**							
Width x height	0.9 m	1.2 m	1.5 m	1.8 m	2.1 m	2.4 m	2.7 m	3 m
SWLs in kilonewtons								
63 x 100 mm	4	3	2	2	2	1.85	1.65	1.5
63 x 220 mm	21	16	13	11	9	8	7	6
100 x 150 mm	27	21	16	14	12	10	9	8
100 x 220 mm	58	45	35	30	26	23	20	18

which is often kept in stock at builders' merchants. However, you can see from the table that it is capable of carrying only very light loads. Across a 3 m opening, for example, it will accept only 1.5 kn, the weight of four or five courses of bricks rendered and plastered, and so you can see that it is really only suited to openings in non-loadbearing walls where only the self-weight of the remaining brickwork above is supported by it.

As a rule, concrete lintels are not suitable in external walls because of cold-bridging. This effect is produced by installing elements into insulated parts of your home, creating a path for heat to escape along. Condensation can also form on the surface of a cold bridge.

Removing chimney breasts

Victorian and Edwardian houses were typically built with a wealth of fireplaces and chimneys. More often than not, the chimney flues run as brick-built projections through the upstairs rooms to the attic (where they often join together) and from there into the rooftop chimney.

The bedrooms they pass through are not always sizeably proportioned, particularly in terraced homes, and every inch of space could be used if the chimney breasts were cut back flush with the wall – if the fireplaces on the ground floor have become redundant through central heating, or have been replaced with balanced flue gas fires, then this can easily be achieved. The attic is the best place to cut back the breast and support what remains above it. Up here above the ceiling line, a

structural bracket or beam can be built in without needing to be boxed in and decorated afterwards.

As a structural alteration, however, this work is subject to control under the Building Regulations, and you will need to make an application. The Building Control Officer's interest lies in ensuring that the weight of the retained chimney is safely supported, and it's a good idea to submit details on how you are planning to do this beforehand for their approval. A Full Plans Application will allow them to examine and approve your details in advance, but you could equally send this information with a Building Notice and ask for it to be examined.

Apart from the usual function of a chimney, chimney breasts have one extra quality, adding a buttressing measure to a wall that might otherwise lack stability. If your home has no internal loadbearing walls supporting a gable end, for example, but a chimney stack, this strengthens the wall like a pier, and removing it could be damaging. A good many Victorian properties do have central loadbearing walls that include chimney breasts rising from two rooms of the gable wall and joining together in the attic, and these can easily be cut back and supported in the roof space. Without the presence of a central loadbearing wall, however, their loss could compromise the stability of the wall, making it vulnerable to wind loads.

Don't forget that whatever the size of the chimney that is left, the flue in it will need to be ventilated if it is to remain dry. Capped flues are sources of damp when the air isn't allowed to flow through them, and so ventilating them is particularly important if some of the structure is left within your room. The most effective way of building in ventilation is to install brick-sized louvred air bricks with a standard 215 x 75 mm vent, at the lowest and highest part of the flue.

How to support brick chimneys

Chimneys are by their very nature hollow. The walls around the flue may be a half a brick or a whole brick thick, but are seldom more. The flue size itself is another matter, but it shouldn't be less than 225 mm square. The point here is that the breast can be measured as a projection that is often at least 450 mm deep, making it a very odd size for supporting.

Gallows brackets are usually the most convenient way of supporting a chimney breast in the roof space. Using 75 mm mild steel angle, pre-drilled to accept expansion bolts and pre-welded into a bracket that is topped with mild steel sheet, they can be fixed to the supporting wall as a structural shelf. There are a few preconditions that should be taken before this method can be adopted, however:

● Check that the height of the chimney retained above the roof is similar to that retained below the roof level. In this way a balance is achieved to maintain stability. This usually means that the bracket is secured just above the ceiling joist level, and not up near the rafters.

● Check that the angles are no greater than 600 mm apart. In practice the most common arrangements consist of three angles for a chimney comprising two flues.

● Check that the wall onto which the bracket is to be bolted is of adequate thickness and condition. A half-brick wall, for example, may suffer from bending when part of the chimney breast has been removed. The method works best with a 215 mm party wall that has a corresponding chimney on the opposite side.

Structural brackets

The key to a structural bracket's success is in its fixings, because it is they that will transfer the weight of the retained chimney in their shear and tensile strength. The expanding bolt is the ideal fixing for any face connection where shear strength is needed; these little devils can be poked into pre-drilled holes and their expanded outer sleeve can be opened up with the turn of the nut-shaped head. I've managed to glamourise this beyond reason, but they do work excitingly well in a hard wall. In a soft block wall they are not so cool.

The other point about bolts is that quantity is usually better than size, because there isn't a great deal of difference in the shear safe working load between an M6 and an M12 bolt, and there are two other sizes between them. The manufacturers will tell you their safe working loads both in shear and tension, and some might even tell you their failure loads when tested right to destruction.

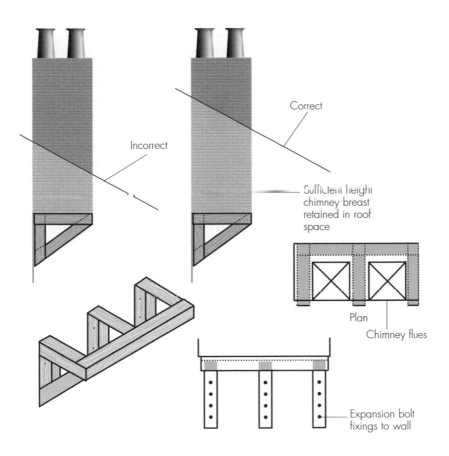

Incorrect

Correct

Sufficient height chimney breast retained in roof space

Plan

Chimney flues

Expansion bolt fixings to wall

Prefabricated steel bracket support to chimney.

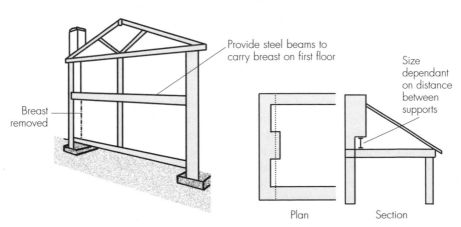

Provide steel beams to carry breast on first floor

Size dependant on distance between supports

Breast removed

Plan

Section

RSJ to support chimney.

73

In a sound brick wall, you might expect an M8 bolt to accept around 1.5 kn in shear load and a bit less in tension. If you space M8 bolts less than 100 mm apart, there will be some reduction in their strength as well. As for the length of the bolt, use nothing longer than will come within 30 mm of the other side of the brickwork. Oh, and try to avoid mortar joints. You were right; I did over-glamourise them.

In addition to mechanically expanding bolts, you can also get chemical anchor bolts, which are ideal for softer walls; a resin solution is injected to the pre-drilled hole, and the bolt is set in.

Replacing a flat roof with a pitched roof

With a tendency to leak, and needing frequent re-covering, flat roofs are seldom appreciated if they can't be used as balconies. So pitching over them with rafters and tiles is popular and can help to improve the appearance of your home and its weather resistance. Single-storey extensions and attached garages are the usual hosts for flat roofs, and sometimes it just isn't possible to create a pitch on it, as first-floor windows on the adjoining walls may be in the way of anything but the most shallow of pitches. Even so, there have been some advances in roof tiles that have made shallow pitches possible. It was once the case that a pitch of 30° was needed for most tiles, and even more for slates, but tile manufacturers now produce tiles that can be laid as low as 12.5° and still be guaranteed against wind uplift and rain. When you consider that anything up to 10° is considered to be a flat roof, you'll realise just how shallow that is. If the aesthetics of your proposal are driving you more than the weather resistance, then I doubt that you'll want anything less than 20°, as even at that angle, tiled roofs can look a little out of sorts. Anything between 30° and 50° will provide you with the widest range of roof coverings and the best in appearance and weather resistance.

Over-roofing like this seems at first glance to be embarrassingly simple: leave the flat roof intact, pitch rafters over it and tile them. There are a few problems that can arise, however, from not stripping off the old roof deck. Condensation can build up beneath it because moist vapour can't penetrate into the new void, vertical restraints can't be installed to the wall plates, if there are any there to start with, and the rafters can't be restrained by the joists if you can't at least cut back the covering and fix between them. All things considered, the flat roof deck is best taken off.

Your new pitched roof is likely to add weight to the walls, and it may be necessary to have the existing lintels and foundations checked to ensure they are good enough to cope with this increase. Typically, this may be in the order of 20–30 per cent heavier, not a huge amount.

There is a good flip side to this extra weight: it will serve to hold the roof down. Your flat roof should have been anchored down with vertical restraint

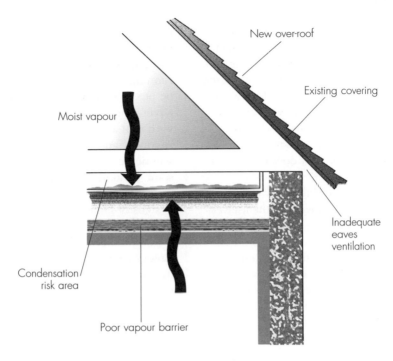

New over-roof

Existing covering

Moist vapour

Inadequate eaves ventilation

Condensation risk area

Poor vapour barrier

Problems with over-roofing.

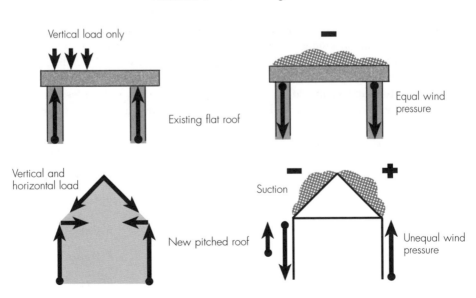

Vertical load only

Existing flat roof

Equal wind pressure

Vertical and horizontal load

New pitched roof

Suction

Unequal wind pressure

Force changes from over-roofing.

straps fixed to the wall plate, but if it wasn't, installing them now is going to mean breaking through the ceiling and chopping out 1 m-long strips of plaster, unless you can rely on the dead weight of the tiles to hold it down. Concrete tiles can do this in most sheltered areas, but fixings may be needed in high-exposure locations. It does help if you have heavy tiles – some types of concrete interlocking tiles weigh in at 50 kg per square metre by themselves and look like paving slabs, so this is not such a tall order.

To combat the risk of condensation in your newly formed roof space, perforated roofing felt can be used, or proprietary vents can be installed at the eaves. With the latter available in 40 varieties, you're bound to find one that looks right – you need at least the equivalent of a 10 mm continuous gap. Some perforated felts are adequate without further ventilation, but you need to check the installing conditions for each product, as some will need counter-battens.

By over-roofing you should undoubtedly have made your roof more resistant to rain, but you will also have increased the roof area and thus the amount of rainfall running off it – and running off it at a higher rate. It may not be possible to retain the existing gutters – half-round 100 mm ones will deal with roof areas of about 37 sq m, but any more and shaped or larger gutters will be needed. I say 'shaped', because some contemporary designs offer much higher flow rates than traditional designs of gutters.

Repairing valleys

Valleys are the intersections between the slopes of two interlinking roofs, the place where rainfall is channelled and where snow can build up; and because of these two issues they are treated as potential problem spots with regard to keeping them watertight. Lead can split with age and solar heat, and once a valley starts to leak, it is best to re-line the bay, if not the whole valley. Valleys can be re-formed and weathered in a few different ways; depending on the tiles you are using, it may also be possible to buy valley tiles, pre-shaped to continue tiling the roof without

LEAD VALLEY DIMENSIONS			
Code	Min step (drip) height	Max length of bay	Max overall girth
4	50 mm	1500 mm	750 mm
5	50 mm	2000 mm	800 mm
6	50 mm	2250 mm	850 mm
7	60 mm	2500 mm	900 mm
8	60 mm	3000 mm	1000 mm

3 Expert Points

HERE ARE THREE EXPERT POINTS FOR
LEAD VALLEYS:

1 Code 4 lead is the minimum grade
for use in gutters, but because the
lengths are limited to only 1.5 m, code 5
is more standard.

2 The minimum fall along lead lined
gutters should be 1:00. Falls of
steeper than 1:60 should receive
improved nail fixings to prevent slippage.

3 Tapered gutters should not be less
than 150 mm wide at their narrowest
or lowest point.

breaking the course or cutting the tiles.
More often the tiles have been cut to
suit the angle of the valley, and the
valley itself is a gutter lined with lead.

Either way, valleys need to be
supported – it isn't sufficient to just let
the tiling battens run over the last rafter
and carry the weight. Timber boards or
plywood are normally used to form a
shuttering base across the rafters and
the valley base.

If the main roof continues through to
wallplates and bearing, then the
intersecting roof may sit on to it using
layboards. These relatively thin softwood
boards are simply plates onto which the
rafters can be cut and nailed.

Because lead suffers from thermal
movement, linings to gutters have to be
formed in pieces with lapped joints and
laid on an underlay that stops it sticking
to the board. The maximum length of
each piece or bay between steps is
related to the thickness (coded by

numbers) and the width or girth. The
table opposite illustrates this.

Glassfibre valleys

GRP (glassfibre) valley troughs are
becoming a popular alternative to
traditional lead linings; although the
material is thin, it may not creep so
much as lead on hot, sunny days. Lead
gutters have one distinctive benefit over
GRP: they allow access for cleaning. You
can walk up them if need be, without
fear of damaging them. Thinner GRP is
likely to split if you tried this, but the
narrower-width polished surface is
going to make it a 'north face of the
Eiger' ascent anyway. All things
considered, it is best to reserve GRP for
steeper and more inaccessible gutters,
such as those at the intersection of
opposing steep roofs.

Moving a staircase

Staircases aren't always in the ideal
place, but we have a tendency to think
that, along with the roof, they can't be
moved and we just have to live with
them where they are. That isn't the case
at all; stairs are easily moved – the hard
bit is deciding where to move them to.

In small Victorian terraced homes,
with two up and two down, the
staircase usually lives in the space in the
middle of the home, where it rises
steeply between matchboarded
partitions. With the ground floor rooms
being so small, creating an open-plan
layout down here can be a popular
improvement, but the stairs divide the
rooms and need to be moved through
90° to run up alongside the wall. In
doing this the stairwell will rob one of

the bedrooms of some floor space, but it will be gained back by flooring over the old stairwell and it should be possible to bring the stairs up to the same landing area. Not only does this conjure up the possibility of spacious open-plan living downstairs, it also brings the stairs down in a better place, often to the front door position, making it far better for access and escape in case of fire.

It's important to set the staircase back from the door swing by at least 400 mm to avoid swiping somebody on the nose when you arrive home. If you have the space, enclosing the staircase within a partition and creating a hallway is ideal. It will serve as a draught lobby to your reception rooms when the front door is in use, and will protect your escape if a fire occurs in them while you are upstairs. If your home is quite narrow and you feel a solid stair partition would create too much of an enclosure, look at creating a safety glass screen and glazed door before you revert to having the stairs within the room itself.

Don't forget that understair space will still exist for a cupboard or an item of furniture, so long as the underside of the stairs is drawn with plasterboard and finished. It is possible to support the partition at the line of the stairs, rather than taking it down to floor level, by installing a beam at the angle of the stairs alongside the string of the staircase and supporting the partition from this. It does requires a bit of structural design work, but beams don't have to be level to work, so long as they are vertically supported at their

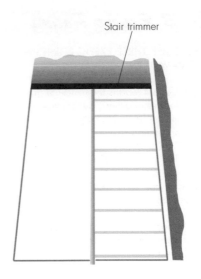

Stair trimmer

Stair trimming

Stairwell plans.

bearings and adequately fixed. A small steel beam, for example, could be used to achieve this with cranked ends at the landings that could provide the bearings. Given light loads, this may be possible in square hollow-section steel tubing that is light to handle and cheap. I haven't actually seen anyone do this, but then I haven't suggested it before, so maybe I will.

Floating stairs can make attractive features, and precast ones are ideal for this, since they can span between floors without the support of walls. They also have the advantage of a limitless range of finishes to clad them with, from paint to tiles and timber to carpet. Structurally, their support to a timber stairwell will need to be designed.

Forming a stairwell

The stairwell is the hole in the floor through which the stairs and you will pass. The majority of homes have timber joist upper floors, and with the boards lifted the joists can be easily cut to create the new stairwell. Obviously the cut joists will need to be temporarily supported from below with adjustable props to allow this to happen.

For the opening in the floor to be permanently supported, it will need to be trimmed. Trimming is done with joists of the same depth, usually doubled up or more, to form a framework around the stairwell. For this to work, the member added to support the cut floor joists has itself to be supported at either end. This member is known as the trimmer, and the one supporting it as the trimming. The trimming joist runs in the same direction as the other floor joists, and in some cases it may need to be a flitch beam or even a steel beam. In this form it will also support a wall on the first floor over a long span.

Today, most staircases occupy about 2.5 m on plan, but since the trimming needs to run to the bearing point, it needs to be considered structurally. The actual size of the stairwell is also determined by the fact that at least 2 m clear headroom should be achieved from the stair below, although you may be able to squeeze a bit out of this figure in consultation with your Building Control Surveyor if space dictates. Hence there is a minimum size for a stairwell, but not a maximum one – the bigger it is, however, the more floor space you lose upstairs.

Trimmer joists are best supported by joist hangars to their trimming members. Hangars are metal shoes that can hook over the joist and be peppered with a number of nail fixings; in doing this, the support is assured and is easier to achieve in a confined space. Hangers don't create the risk of split wood that happens all too frequently with thumping in 75 mm nails.

It is possible for the newel posts of staircases to become structural members and support the stairwell trimming, but the drawback is with the size of timber needed. For any member structurally supporting the floor, fire resistance is needed on top of the ability to carry the load, and a timber newel will need to be oversized to achieve this, making it look more like the independent post it is, rather than part of the staircase. You can expect at least to have to use a 150 x 150 mm PAR post, if not bigger, and support it at the base effectively.

Stair design

Stairs are dangerous places and have been subjected to dimensional controls for a long time to make them safer. The rise and going is the term given for the steps and treads, and these dimensions should be equal throughout the stairs. A sudden change in them will throw you off your footing and induce a fall. The maximum rise is 220 mm and the minimum going is 220 mm, but the relationship between the two should not create a pitch of more than 42°. The formula of twice the rise plus once the going should also fall in between 550 mm and 700 mm when added up.

Chances are you that will have to order a purpose-made staircase to fit your home, given its floor-to-floor height and these requirements, but if you are lucky, standard staircases are available off the shelf to suit standard (read modern mass-built) ceiling heights. The latter are, of course, considerably cheaper than the custom-made ones.

Stairs also need handrails on at least one side of the flight and around the stairwell on the landing. These are sited at a height of 900 mm. If you've always thought there should be the potential for a lot of design input with balustrading, but never see it, this is likely due to regulations – spindles have to be less than 100 mm apart and vertical, or at least diagonal (to prevent small boys climbing them in between kicking the skirting boards and thumping the doors).

Totally infilling stairs with boarding of any kind looks like a rewind to the 1960s, when everyone was encouraged to hardboard over their wood panel doors, but there is no reason why a suitable laminated glass couldn't be used as infill or, come to that, a dwarf wall couldn't be built. The ship's rail look, with taut horizontal wires, is popular with minimalists, but doesn't seem to comply with Building Regulations as it can be easily climbed by children.

Installing a rooflight

It never ceases to amaze me how much light you can bring in through one window in the roof. A small rooflight can illuminate the darkest of places, and it's often worth installing one to serve the attic alone. Even if you only use it for maintenance, a rooflight for natural light will make looking for spare light bulbs so much easier.

Manufacturers sometimes sell single-glazed units of a reduced standard and price for this very use, if you don't want to run to the expense of the latest double-glazed units. What seems hard to find (in 2003 at any rate) is a fixed rooflight that brings in daylight but no ventilation. I presume the market for these must be too small to warrant their manufacture.

Consents

While installing a rooflight in your loft is not likely to need Planning Permission – I said a rooflight, not a dormer window, by the way – it usually needs Building Regulation Approval. This is because the work often involves cutting one or more of the rafters and trimming out a structural opening for the window. Those trimmings are the equivalent of lintels above the windows in your walls, and have to be checked to ensure they are adequate. The job is defined as a Material Alteration, a phrase which has entirely nothing to do with the materials being used.

If you are installing a small rooflight between the rafters and no cutting of the roof structure is needed, you are accordingly exempt from Building Regulation controls under the Building Regulations 2000.

Installation

Cut-and-pitched roofs are easily adapted to house rooflights: the felt can be sliced open and the rafters cut and trimmed, with a doubled-up trimmer taken to a doubled-up trimming at either side, in just the same way that a stairwell is trimmed.

Sometimes it may be impractical, if not actually impossible, to get an extra rafter alongside the existing ones, and it might prove easier to install a purlin to reduce their span. It's also worth considering whether a doubled-up trimming rafter is actually necessary. If your rooflight is very high up on the roof near to the ridge, it may not have much load to support on the trimmer, and so not much is carried to the rafters either side. It helps enormously if your home was built with substantial rafters, as older properties with 50 x 100 mm rafters usually are; modern standard rafters are overstressed to start with, and any roof window is going to make them worse.

If your roof is a trussed-rafter type, installing the rooflight between trusses is the easiest solution. At 600 mm centres for most trusses, some of the smaller models are able to fit snugly between them without cutting the trusses. With trussed rafters, it is not possible to cut and trim around the opening as you would with a cut-and-pitched roof – their slender timbers have been designed into a webbed shape that relies upon it staying intact for structural stability, and a trimming arrangement would have to be designed by the manufacturer or a structural engineer to overcome this.

Weathering

As well as the rooflight itself, you will also need to buy a flashing kit to ensure weather resistance. A lot of work and experience has gone into developing flashings that will fit snugly to any type of roof covering – so long as you obtain the right one. For example, there is a difference usually between tiles with corrugations of up to 45 mm and those with deeper rolls, in the French farmhouse style.

With the window frame fixed into position, the window itself is removed by its hinge pins, and a soaker collar is clipped in and dressed over the felt and battens beneath the tiles. Collars seal to all four sides of the window, although when the tiles are fixed back on, a flashing is secured over the top and dressed (pressed to the shape of the tiles) over the tiling beneath the window. The top and side flashings have pre-formed channels for the rainwater to run down.

At long last in 2002 a manufacturer introduced white polyurethane-finished rooflights instead of bare wood. These will actually blend in with the UPVC windows and doors many of our homes now have, and the rooflight no longer has to be the only odd-looking window. Hopefully one day the option will exist to buy UPVC versions instead of timber coated with plastic.

When is a loft conversion not a loft conversion?

Popular false answers include, when it isn't a bedroom, and when it's only a hobby room, but both are wrong. It's a popular myth that loft conversions only occur when the attic is being turned into a bedroom, but that isn't the case. Any kind of a room will change it from an attic for access and light storage to an occupied space, and will invoke the requirements of the Building Regulations. Building Control Officers and Conveyance Surveyors will be forced to make a judgement on the status of a loft by inspection, and there are no general rules.

It is in my view acceptable to install a window or simple lighting to a loft and lay some decking boards for access and light storage; beyond that, you are on your own. If you plaster the walls or rafters, install a fixed stair or ladder and add power points, then most people will read it as a loft conversion that should be controlled by the Regulations, and not having gone through that process will likely mean applying for Regularisation.

Unauthorised loft conversions are now being revealed frequently since legal professionals have discovered that they carry some liability for conveyancing a home without the necessary approvals, and few unauthorised conversions escape attention forever.

CHAPTER 5

Non–Structural Alterations

Plumbing alterations

Technological advances in heating and hot-water systems have made upgrading the plumbing in our homes both possible and worthwhile. I don't think either was feasible before the 1990s, but as every year passes, technology in this trade leaps forward in one respect or another. Our homes may look the same, but the heating and the storage and management of our hot water has improved quite a bit in the last decade or so. For what seemed like ages, builders persisted with the tried and tested system of indirect vented hot water that was gravity-fed from tanks in the loft space. Not any more – unvented pressurised systems are becoming the standard for new homes, and can deliver large quantities of hot water on demand, running multiple baths and showers and dishwashers simultaneously. Altering your home's plumbing systems can allow you to meet those demands for today and to anticipate for tomorrow.

Replacing a boiler

In the first instance, you can increase the speed at which your home is heated from a standing cold start. It used to take a couple of hours to heat my home with a 1987 fitted gas balanced flue boiler, but now with a 2002 fitted gas balanced flue combi boiler it reaches optimum temperature inside half an hour. I have tested this by inadvertently shutting the heating down for 36 hours during sub-zero January weather with a loose roomstat connection. It was impressive at how quickly it could return the place to a warm 25° in each room from what seemed like a permanent chill. Before this we'd had to use a programmer with a holiday setting that would wake the boiler up the day before we were due home – how energy-efficient was that?

My choice of a combi was for a particular reason – it gave the opportunity to convert the airing cupboard in the bathroom, which was previously home to a hot water cylinder, pump, and pipework and valves, into a shower cubicle. With combi boilers, all the storage problems associated with keeping hot water and circulating it disappear, because the boiler has its own built-in pump and functions by roomstat or programmer to supply heating and to supply hot water by demand from the taps. Inside, there is a flow switch that triggers the boiler's ignition once the flow from an open tap reaches a factory-set amount (around 4 l per minute).

The latest boilers can run with efficiencies of 95 per cent compared to the 60 or 70 per cent of 1980s models. Condensing boilers come top of the list: by using heat exchangers to cool exhaust gases, the flue pipes can be made of plastic, and they run at much lower temperatures, wasting very little heat.

Cost

So replacing your boiler with a condensing model can save you money in the long-term on fuel bills, but combis are still relatively expensive to buy and install, and the cash-back grants that were available when they first appeared seemed to have become scarce. Steer well clear of any companies who 'quote' for the work of replacement with a 'grant-aid' discount included – if there are any grants for a product on offer, you want to receive them direct. Now they are in competition for everything, even the main gas service companies run scams, and quite often they contract out such work to plumbing firms.

In terms of the initial expense, it really helps to have an extra reason for upgrading. Maybe your existing boiler is aged and the parts are no longer available, or it has begun to rust, or you want a quieter model, or a smaller one to hide inside a kitchen unit.

Choosing a boiler

The quietest boilers are those with cast-iron casings, and they really are quiet, so much so that it is difficult to tell if they are running at all. If your boiler is located in the living parts of your home, it means a lot that it doesn't run like a tractor after being jump-started. The drawback with cast-iron cased boilers is predictable – they are very, very heavy. With a wall-mounted model you need to know that your walls are suited to heavyweight fixings. I have yet to see a combi boiler with a cast-iron case, perhaps because it would weigh even more.

The other good option you have with boilers is their size. The rated output that you need doesn't seem to be affected by this factor. Even combi boilers with 120,000 Btu ratings can fit snugly into a kitchen wall cupboard –

yes, they are tightly engineered and maintenance has to be carried out by Japanese midwives, but the only bit you need to get to is the filling loop, which is fitted below. The critical dimension is the depth: 500 mm is the standard wall unit depth, and of course you need to allow a nominal gap between the cupboard door and the boiler face.

With balanced flue boilers, the fitted depth of the appliance can vary with the options for the flue position. The details of most boilers and these critical dimensions can be obtained from the maker's website and plumbers' merchants before you buy. With balanced flue boilers, you only need to get at the boiler for servicing, so the door needs to fully reveal the front of the boiler so you can remove the case panel and the underside. If you can fit the doors to just the side and top panels of the cupboard, it will help.

Finding a fitter

The work of replacing a boiler is a controlled service under the Building Regulations. In this way it is regulated to approved tradesmen who can self-certify their own work. With gas boilers, a CORGI-registered fitter will be able to do this, and with oil boilers, an OFTEC-registered fitter. On completion they should provide a commissioning certificate, completed with their registration numbers and the details of the boiler and its controls. Part of the process of commissioning is also fully explaining how the controls work to the home owner, so make sure they don't simply hand over the manual to you.

Plumbers are infamous for their lack

of care around buildings. A new boiler means draining down the system, and your plumber will want to run a hosepipe into your garden, where the contaminated water of the heating system will end plant life for years. It will likely need new holes through the wall for drain overflow pipes or flues, and you can expect any plumber to bore through from the inside. This should blow the face off your bricks in the same way that exit wounds from gunshots are worse than entry wounds. To a plumber, the trail of destruction is all part of the 'making good' that some other person must do in their wake. If they have a trade logo, it must be the Latin equivalent of 'You can't make an omelette without breaking a few eggs… and the frying pan, denting the cooker and oiling the floor.'

If you do find a plumber who shows respect for your home, cherish him and recommend him to others.

Upgrading heating and hot water controls

Programmers

In the UK we have always controlled our heating and hot water needs by time switches – programmers – but in Scandinavia they don't know what a programmer is. Their heating is on all year round 24 hours a day, but the running temperature is adjusted by room or outside temperature thermostats. They don't see why we would want to switch the boiler on and off at timed intervals during the day.

I think my old neighbour must have been Scandinavian, because when we first had central heating installed to our homes he was adamant that leaving it on permanently was more economical than switching it on and off four times a day. This was 1975, and the back boiler fitted in the old fireplace was controlled by a noisy clock on the wall. He may have been ahead of his time because the programmer controls that were fitted then are only now looking antique.

If your home has an old analogue programmer, you might want to swap it for something a lot more advanced. The fiddly little pins you had to push in and out of the clockface are no longer needed – digital programmers mean only pushing buttons to set your times.

Heating and hot water in conventional systems usually have separate timers on programmers, and you can expect to have at least six times for each a day. Seven-day programmers don't give you the option of having separate times at weekends of course, and now the most basic have five- and two-day programmes to meet your weekend needs. Some will have a holiday setting that allows you to switch off the heating for any number of days when you go away. Instead of having a neighbour pop in the day before your return to switch on and get the place warmed up, the programmer takes care of this for you. This feature could soon be advanced by programmers that receive instructions by telephone, modem or text message, giving total flexibility. When you think of it, there are insurance restrictions on leaving your home empty for too long in the winter for fear of burst water pipes, but controls can take care of that now with frost sensers.

Thermostats

The first thermostats were clock-style roomstats and I am amazed to find mass-home builders still installing them. Invariably they are placed on the living room wall and allow you to set the temperature of the room. Once the heating has brought the temperature of the room up to the desired setting, the roomstat sends a signal down its wire to the boiler, switching it off. Roomstats usually have only two thin control wires and, as I've found to my cost, you need to run them carefully where they can't be pinched or loosened.

Analogue roomstats should have had their day by now – and if it weren't for cheapskate builders, they would have. Digital roomstats are far neater and easier to adjust, and several can be installed within different zones of your home. Zone 1 is always the living room, but zone 2 should be the bedrooms; other zones might be the hall and landing and so on.

Most of our radiators now have individual thermostatic valves. If yours don't, it's an easy task to fit them, and they can be incorporated with roomstats. TRVs (thermostatic radiator valves) became popular in the 1980s, but the trouble with them is that they are simply flow restrictors and tend to stick with use. A thin metal pin is pushed down when the valve is closed, but it can stay down when it's opened and often the valves have to be dismantled and the pin has to be tapped free. If you have a repeat offender, my advice is to chuck it and buy another – I've spent way too much time lying on the floor tapping valves.

Optimum start controls

I have to say this sooner or later, but we all know what our problem is in the UK don't we? The weather. It can be freezing cold one day and blazing hot the next, sometimes it can change as dramatically on the same day, and trying to second-guess what it's going to do is the British obsession. With our heating controls we have always had to assume the worst and wake the boiler up in good time, assuming it will meet with a frosty morning. Of course, this is fine when it does, but for much of the time it doesn't, and the heating has overcooked the home before we've woken, wasting heat and our money. Some weather records indicate that this happens three-quarters of the time, so what we really need is a thermostatic control that takes account of the outside temperature as well – this kind is known generically as an optimum start control.

The simplest optimum start controls have a time delay that takes account of the ambient temperature. All you have to do with these is make sure you set

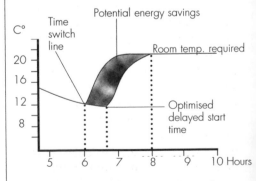

Optimum start controls save energy by ensuring the heating does not come on earlier than necessary.

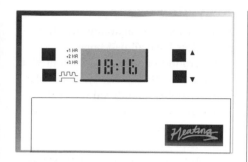

Digital programmable thermostat.

the programmer times to allow for a
delayed start-up on the coldest of days,
meaning you set it to come on early as
you would on a frosty morning, and the
device will kick in when the
temperature is warmer and delay the
boiler ignition. The warmer it is, the
longer it delays the start-up.

You can improve on that by buying a
programmable roomstat. I am very
excited by this gadget, although I
concede to having a low threshold of
excitement following too many years in
local government. Instead of setting on-
off times with a programmer, these
devices let you programme in desired
temperatures for different times of the
day. It's a programmer and roomstat all
in one, so you don't need another
programmer. Again, it is best to get one
which recognises the weekends and lets
you have different settings for them. The
temperature range usually runs from
5–30°C, so you could set it low at night
and very low when you go away on
holiday, to keep the chill off the place.
Some programmable roomstats have a
self-learning facility that lets them adjust
to your home, avoiding long periods of
pre-heating in cold weather.

Weather compensators

I know what you're thinking – anything
called a weather compensator must be
worth its weight in gold. Compensators
are extensions of optimum start-ups and
seek to balance the fact that the rate of
heat loss from your home is partly due
to its construction and insulation, and
partly due to what the temperature is
outside. On cold days the heat escapes a
lot quicker than on mild days.

In domestic heating, we have BEM
(Boiler Energy Management) devices
that add this extra level of control. I'm
on your side – weather compensator
sounds much better, but maybe the
Department of Acronyms couldn't use
another WC. The device adjusts the
response rate ratio between the boiler
and outside air temperature, and the
end result is that the radiators don't get
so hot when it's warm outside, and the
comfortable temperature you want is
achieved without a furnace of heat
coming off part of the wall. You can't
use a roomstat with one of these, but
you can still have TRVs on the radiators.
This system meets the Building
Regulation requirement for a boiler
interlock that stops the boiler firing
when heat isn't needed.

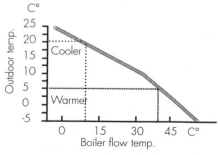

Graph showing the benefits of Boiler Energy
Management (or weather compensator).

Boiler Energy Manager.

You can add a BEM device to an existing system almost as easily as you can add optimum start controls, and the really great thing about upgrading your plumbing system with them is that you don't need a plumber. A heating engineer would be useful, but these are dry-side controls that don't involve cutting pipes or anything to do with water, and the fear of leaks that dissuades even plumbers from plumbing doesn't apply. You don't even have to drain the system down, and once BEMs are fitted you can forget about them.

Saving water

The cheapest thing you can do is add a water hippo to your toilet cistern. Water hippos are not large aquatic mammals equipped with huge teeth and bad tempers, but plastic bags that retain some of the water when the loo is flushed. Thus they reduce its flush volume, useful if you're metered and have an older 2 gal (9 l) model. If you were changing the bathroom suite for a new one anyway, a brand-new WC now comes with a smaller 6 l cistern or dual-flush mechanism to comply with current Water Regulations.

Recycling water

I have worked in an area where the properties have all had huge underground rainwater tanks built with them in the 1930s – beautiful, circular brick chambers, rendered waterproof inside and with pipes to draw up the water into the kitchens. These aren't wells – they are only 3 m deep – but rainwater storage tanks (below-ground water butts) fed by the gutters and downpipes off the roofs. Each bungalow has its own, and all are but a few feet from the back door. I know this because every time an owner wants to extend one it has to be built over. Nobody yet has expressed an interest in re-employing it. Many were only backfilled in the 1980s, when patios were laid over the top. Backfill material is archaeology at its best: empty beer cans with sell-by dates, supermarket plastic bags – most of our modern-day rubbish is dateable, and it must have seemed to some home-owners, where better to put it than in your own little landfill site?

I'm sure the tanks were built at a time of necessity, but perhaps that time will return. With so many new homes being built to house a growing population in parts of Britain, the demand for water is becoming unreasonably high. In future drought years, having your own water reservoir may come to prove invaluable.

Recycling some of the water we use is something that we could all benefit from, but it is not without its difficulties. I'll be straight with you here, I'm not sure whether it would be cost-effective for the unmetered without your water company giving you some

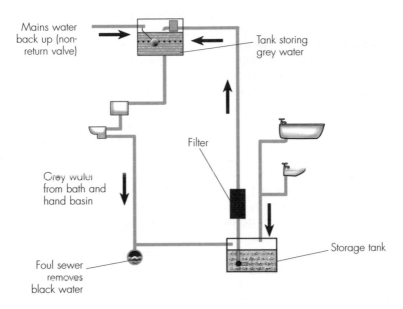

Grey water recycling system.

cash benefit for recycling. I think they should; after all, the water authorities who own the drainage sewers have been giving discounts to those of us who discharge our rainwater to soakaways, so why not?

The logistics of recycling water

The major problem here is the health one. In 21st-century Britain the authorities take a dim view of anyone mucking about with the water supply and accidentally contaminating it. Our drinking (and cooking) water, or potable water as it's known, has to be kept separate from any treating, recycling or softening that you might want to do. The sad thing is that it only represents 5 per cent of our water

consumption; the remaining 95 per cent is employed in washing (whether it be us, clothes or dishes), WCs, cleaning and gardening. Foul water has always been the term applied to all of this, but now we really have to break it down into shades – shades of foulness if you like.

Dealing with the really foul stuff (known as black water) from our WCs is, of course, the hardest, and frankly not many of us would want to try recycling this. Once the cistern handle is pulled, we rather like the idea of it being somebody else's problem. The bath and sink water, on the other hand, have definite possibilities. Cleaning water like this has become known as grey water, and grey water can be easily cleaned and recycled for use again. When you consider that our present and rapidly increasing rate of water consumption is likely to continue for the foreseeable future, water rationing and controls could become part of our daily lives. Installing a grey-water handling system in your home doesn't sound like a bad idea, so what are you going to need?

For recycling water for use in toilets and in washing (non-potable water), first and foremost you are going to need a storage tank to which your grey water can be discharged. It will need to be of sufficient capacity to meet your needs, but a fibreglass tank buried in the garden could have an overflow pipe connecting it to your foul drainage system should it begin to overfill. The waste pipes from your kitchen sink, wash hand basins, bath and shower, and even from your washing machine and dishwasher, can all be connected to one drain supplying this tank. A filter tank en-route serves to remove the worst of the soap and detergents before it gets to the main tank.

Once in the main tank the water can be sterilised with bleach and pumped via a 22 mm plastic water pipe back into the home. The electric-powered pump needs to be capable of raising the water to the loft and a delivery tank, where it can be stored again for imminent use. A disinfectant block in this tank will serve to clean the water again until it is gravity-supplied on demand from the appliances that it came from. If this is backed up by a mains feed for emergencies or to top up the water system, your home's hygiene requirements could be guaranteed as met. All of this needs to be separate

from the potable water system, so in effect you are doubling up on the plumbing in your home.

These systems aren't the daydream of a half-mad building inspector, but are available today; I just don't think many people will use them until the financial rewards become obvious. Even without a water company rebate, if you have a sealed cesspool system serving your foul drainage that costs you so much a year to have emptied, then you could reduce this cost by a staggering proportion with such a system.

Drawing your own potable water

This currently relies upon you having your own private borehole to an aquifer or spring. Even then it may need filtering and treating with UV light to remove bacteria. Private water supplies have to be sample-tested regularly, a task usually deferred to local authority Environmental Health Officers, before it can be judged fit for consumption.

Adding solar power

This is beyond the line as far as many green crusades go, but it's worth mentioning because at long last solar power is starting to be sensible - meaning that it fits in with our homes and actually works. For decades it's been with us and has completely and utterly failed to impress anyone. If you've seen the occasional house sporting a solar panel on its roof, you'll understand why: what appears from a distance to be a commercial greenhouse propagator bolted on top of a south-facing roof slope, looks close up like a commercial greenhouse propagator bolted on top....And not only did they appear ugly and detached from the design of the house, but the things worked by solar heating water pipes, meaning that they really needed sunshine to get enough heat, so for three Thursdays in July you could produce enough hot water from solar power to run a bath – whether you wanted one or not.

In the same way that the motor-car engine has been slow to evolve, solar power has too, but the first steps have been made: at last you can buy solar roof tiles that fit on your roof alongside the others, flush with the roof line and neat-looking. They are sold by tile manufacturers who have produced them to actually fit alongside their standard tiles – and here's the astounding thing: they are photo-voltaic (PV) and work on UV light. UV, or ultraviolet light is available even on cloudy days, making the tiles efficient even in Britain. I would like to say that they look indistinguishable from ordinary tiles, but they have a glassy purplish look to them that only starts to blend in when used alongside slates of a similar colour.

Even so, I have a good feeling about PV technology, and I'm sure that it won't be long before we'll all be adding solar tiles to our roofs and reducing our electricity bills. For those of you going over the line, the DTI have offered 50 per cent grants for PV installations to get the ball rolling for the rest of us. Like all technology, the price will come down given time and enough demand.

Electrical alterations

Strange as it might seem given the increasing demand for electrical power in our homes, the incidence of electric shock fatalities has been falling since the 1970s. But the non-fatal shock rate has increased, particularly in the 1990s, along within our ownership of electrical appliances. From 1990–98 there were only five fatalities but 576 non-fatal incidents recorded from fixed installations, but from electrical appliances this rose to 14 deaths and 1,700 non-fatal injuries. Either we are getting more careless and yet more lucky with it, or we own more appliances now. Either way plans exist to increase the number of quality electrical installations in our homes, installed by registered professionals.

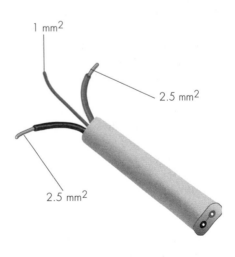

1 mm^2

2.5 mm^2

2.5 mm^2

Twin and earth cable with 1mm^2 earth core.

According to the VAT register, up until 2004 about half the electricians trading in the UK have been fully qualified and registered with the recognised bodies, leaving the other half to be described as anything from 'jobbing' electricians to 'cowboys', depending on their quality and your point of view. When you add in the tradesmen who aren't VAT-registered, the fraction must increase to at least three-quarters.

Electrical hardware can, and no doubt will, always be purchasable from DIY shops for homeowners to install themselves, so has it been a problem? The government must have thought so, because plans to include electrical safety under a new part of the Building Regulations now exist. In bringing in these controls for the first time ever in England and Wales, they aim to reduce the number of electric shock fatalities by 20 per cent and non-fatalities by up to 10 per cent. Fires caused by electrical installations have qualified at about the 20 per cent mark, so it is hoped that these measures will make our homes much safer.

For electricians the recognised bodies are the NICEIC (National Inspection Council for Electrical Installation Contracting) and the ECA (Electrical Contractors Association), and you should look for a contractor that is registered with either. In employing them, a certificate of testing and compliance with the relevant standards of safety and quality will be available to you for any work they do. This is particularly beneficial when it's 'notifiable work' under the Building Regulations. Notifiable work could mean adding extra power sockets or light points, and only a suitably qualified electrician (registered with the NICEIC or the ECA) will be able to self-certify the work and avoid a Building Control Service application.

If you do plan to do the work yourself or use an unregistered electrician, it will certainly pay to have it inspected and tested by a qualified electrician once you've finished. Two different certificates are available: one is for new circuits, such as to an extension, and the other is for minor electrical work like alterations.

Minor Electrical Installation Works Certificate

Electricians engaged in alteration work to the electrical system of your home should issue you with a certificate of compliance on completing the work. For minor alterations that haven't involved the creation of a new circuit, an example of the type of certificate and the information on it is shown on page 93. It should include a description of the work, installation details, what tests were carried out, and a declaration of its compliance with the British Standard and the IEE Wiring Regulations as well.

You should be in receipt of the original certificate, and your electrician should keep the duplicate copy. It's an important document to place in your home logbook. It should illustrate compliance with the IEE Wiring Regulations which cover electrical work in detail. In the future, it is highly likely that you will need to declare it if you

Form 5

MINOR ELECTRICAL INSTALLATION WORKS CERTIFICATE
(REQUIREMENTS FOR ELECTRICAL INSTALLATIONS - BS 7671 [IEE WIRING REGULATIONS])
To be used only for minor electrical work which does not include the provision of a new circuit

---

PART 1 : Description of minor works

1. Description of the minor works : ....

2. Location/Address : ....

3. Date minor works completed : ....

4. Details of departures, if any, from BS 7671

....

....

....

PART 2 : Installation details

1. System earthing arrangement: TN-C-S ☐   TN-S ☐   TT ☐

2. Method of protection against indirect contact: ....

3. Protective device for the modified circuit :   Type BS ....   Rating .... A

4. Comments on existing installation, including adequacy of earthing and bonding arrangements : (see Regulation 130-07)

....

....

....

PART 3 : Essential Tests
1. Earth continuity : satisfactory   ☐

2. Insulation resistance:
           Phase/neutral .... $M\Omega$

           Phase/earth .... $M\Omega$

           Neutral/earth .... $M\Omega$

3. Earth fault loop impedance .... Ω

4. Polarity : satisfactory   ☐

5. RCD operation (if applicable) : Rated residual operating current $I_{\Delta n}$ ....mA and operating time of ....ms (at $I_{\Delta n}$)

PART 4 : Declaration

1. I/We CERTIFY that the said works do not impair the safety of the existing installation, that the said works have been designed, constructed, inspected and tested in accordance with BS 7671 : .... (IEE Wiring Regulations), amended to .... and that the said works, to the best of my/our knowledge and belief, at the time of my/our inspection, complied with BS 7671 except as detailed in Part 1.

2. Name: ....   3. Signature: ....

   For and on behalf of: ....   Position: ....

   Address: ....

   ....   Date: ....

   ....

ever sell your home or re-mortgage it. Landlords have had to provide certificates of inspection and testing of electrical circuits for some time, and it may not be long before the same applies to anyone selling a property.

Adding power sockets to an existing circuit is often necessary: most of our homes weren't built with nearly enough socket points to meet our needs today, and adding new ones is far better than running out copious amounts of extension leads.

Double-socket and single-socket outlets have been standard for a long time, but some triple units with fuses built in (similar to extension leads) are also available. For dry-lined walls, such as studwork partitions, plastic dry-lining boxes can be used instead of metal ones. These have the advantage of not needing a fixing into the studs. A correctly cut hole in the plasterboard is essential, however, as they push fit into place. They are a bit more expensive and less robust than the metal patresses, so treat them carefully and don't try to tighten a cross-threaded screw when you come to fix the covers on, or they may split.

Inspection and Testing is a course by itself for qualified electricians, and not all of them are registered in this capacity. In 2003 the pass rate was quoted as only 50 per cent, and many tradesmen in this field simply don't wish to get trained in this area. Their meters are subject to frequent calibration checks, and the work is slow and laborious, involving methodically breaking down circuits and taking readings at set points. I've heard it said

that to speed the job up a bit, it isn't unknown for some to guess at readings and note them in the certificates.

Electrical plans and diagrams

When extending or altering your electrical circuits, planning the layout is critical. Don't leave it to your electrician to advise you on what you want. Think about your needs for lighting as well as power, and whether uplighters or downlighters would suit them best.

A floor plan layout with your light points and power points colour-coded will help you decide, but you will also need to make special note of the height of any points you want over work areas or furniture. Pay special attention to where you want the switches for lights; this isn't always obvious, so give yourself time to plan.

When the work is finished it makes sense to obtain or draw up your own diagram. This isn't an overdrawn plan of each room or floor of your home, but a schematic layout that should be easily reproduced on a sheet of A4 or A3 paper. Take a look at the example shown on page 95, which covers many of the commonly found features in homes and describes them with pictograms. With a completed diagram, you or any future owner of the property should be able to quickly see how the circuits are divided up and what they serve. For example, in the illustration you can see that the stair light is served by two single-pole switches connected to the first-floor lighting circuit, and that the garage is served by a radial circuit leading to a separate consumer unit out

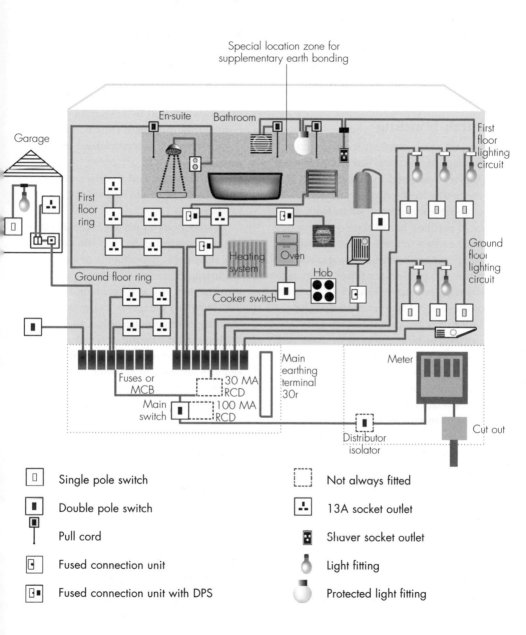

Special location zone for supplementary earth bonding

Garage

En-suite   Bathroom

First floor lighting circuit

First floor ring

Ground floor ring

Heating system   Oven   Hob

Cooker switch

Ground floor lighting circuit

Fuses or MCB

Main switch

30 MA RCD

100 MA RCD

Main earthing terminal 30r

Meter

Cut out

Distributor isolator

	Single pole switch		Not always fitted
	Double pole switch		13A socket outlet
	Pull cord		Shaver socket outlet
	Fused connection unit		Light fitting
	Fused connection unit with DPS		Protected light fitting

Typical home electrical installation.

95

there. The diagram also defines the equipment within the 'special location' zone of the bathroom, where supplementary earth bonding is present. These diagrams, not your plans, should be included in your home logbook with any certificates.

Earth bonding

Correct earth bonding is an essential element of electrical safety, and tests can be conducted to determine its continuity. In the majority of homes, the earthing arrangement stems from the main earthing bar in the consumer unit. Only earth wires acting as the main equipotential bonding may run to metal water and gas service pipes, often at the point of the supply entry. The thickness of these wires was increased in the 1980s. It is not permitted for installation earthing to be connected to these and hasn't been since 1966, prior to which water pipes were used.

While all the circuits will have earth wires connecting back to the main bar, special zones like bathrooms should have extra bonding attached to water pipes, metal heating pipes, metal baths and basins and other exposed conductive parts. The combination of water and electricity is a lethal one, and the opportunity for electricity to short out through metal pipework and await the touch of wet hands is an extremely dangerous one.

Examples of tests that should be carried out on installations include:

● Continuity test

● Polarity test

● Earth fault loop impedence test

● RCD function test

RCDs

Before 1981, voltage-operated circuit breakers were used, recognised by their on-off switch and two separate earth connection terminals. They had the disadvantage of being disabled by a parallel earth path occurring between the connections, and so now only current-operated devices are used, known as RCDs.

Residual circuit breakers are installed to guard against defects in the circuits and thus prevent accidents or fires occurring. Sensitive to changes in the current they trip out, breaking the circuit, when defects occur, cutting off the supply instantaneously. Outdoor wiring was at first the only place we saw them, and then only as plug-in devices for our lawnmowers, given our propensity for mowing through the cable. But now we have hardwired RCDs that can be installed to protect any circuit, and consumer units that come attached with RCDs ready to disconnect the entire home at a moment's notice. My only fear with these is that you can all too frequently be plunged into darkness, so leave plenty of torches around.

Running new cables through old walls

Surface wiring encased in surface conduits has the advantage of being horribly visible, and in that way, safe – nobody is ever going to whang a nail through them to hang a picture hook.

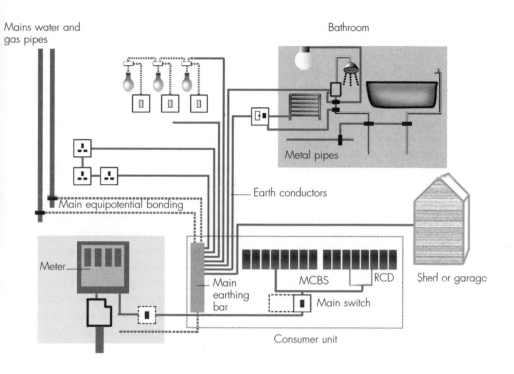

Mains water and
gas pipes

Bathroom

Main equipotential bonding

Earth conductors

Metal pipes

Meter

Main
earthing
bar

MCBS

RCD

Main switch

Shed or garage

Consumer unit

Earth and bonding conductors.

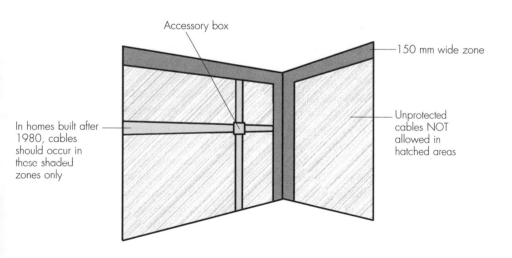

Accessory box

150 mm wide zone

In homes built after
1980, cables
should occur in
these shaded
zones only

Unprotected
cables NOT
allowed in
hatched areas

Hidden cables in walls.

97

They have the disadvantage of being horribly visible – occasionally you see a whole home that has been rewired with surface wires and boxes, and it has suffered an injustice because of it.

The work of chasing in and concealing cables is an important one in my book, and should only be skimped on inside cupboards and the like that are out of sight. New cables don't have to be buried deep; metal protective conduits are thin covers that can be fixed over them once a narrow chase in the wall plaster has been cut and the cable laid in. For studwork walls, the cables can pass through the cavity to boxes without protection within the zone width of the fitting box and in straight lines from it. It makes sense to use a stud and cable detector when tracing existing ones. If your home was built prior to 1980, this measure becomes essential, as before then cables could be run at all angles inside cavities – and often were.

Upgrading smoke alarms

Apart from adding power points and extra lighting, there is another worthwhile improvement you can make to your electrical installation: smoke alarms. The battery-powered ones have done a great job, but you need an army of batteries to keep several alive – and the will power to replace them. Time has proved that many of us haven't. By changing them for mains-powered models, we can save ourselves an unnecessary worry.

Powered alarms don't necessarily need a separate circuit, as those with a rechargeable battery backup can be served by the lighting circuit. They are distinctly louder than battery models, and have the advantage of being able to be interlinked so that when one goes off they all go off. To achieve this use the recommended four-core wire to connect them together; you can always add extra alarms later.

Installing broadband and cable ducts

If you are taking on the task of rewiring or if your alteration work involves exposing floor joists and walls, you can take the opportunity to bring in some ducting to points in your home. You could call it future-proofing – I like this term – which means going that extra bit further now to save you having to make a terrible mess later. While the floors are up you can lay ducts through them for broadband cables or extra standard phone lines now, even if you don't have a need for the service and its cables yet.

Very soon new homes may have to be built with cable ducts and provisions for broadband. If your home has some when this happens, it will bring your property up to competing standard.

Drainage alterations
Connections to existing drains

Connecting up new drainage to existing is easier now than it's ever been. Most private drainage systems laid since the 1980s are in shallow access plasticware. The pipes themselves can be easily cut with a handsaw, and Y junctions can be added with slip collars to connect in new pipework to the system. The worst part is having to dig a big enough hole to work in. If you have UPVC inspection

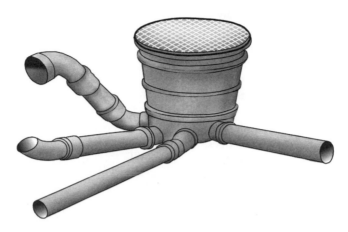

UPVC inspection chamber system.

chambers, the task is even easier, because these preformed units come with entry points for pipes that are blanked off and ready to be opened.

Still common in London and popular elsewhere up to the mid-1980s, clay pipes are a little harder, and electric disc cutters are needed to cut the pipe. Proprietary pipe-cutting tools are for cutting new drainage pipes before laying them, and are not usable in a small trench on a laid pipe. If it proves too awkward to fit a slip collar, flexible rubber sleeve connectors with stainless steel jubilee-type bands will join all types of pipe together painlessly.

Manhole connections in clay pipe systems are harder, since the chambers are either brick or precast concrete with a cement benching around the channel. It is not OK to simply crash the new pipe through a hole in the wall and let the drainage drop into the channel below, but many builders will attempt this. To do the job properly takes more time than that. First, the new

pipe will need a coupling within 600 mm of the manhole wall to keep it flexible. Then it should be brought in at the correct height to join at invert level to the channel. This means having to chop out at least some of the benching to accept a new slipper channel into the direction of flow of the main channel, and then of course to re-form the benching to suit.

Y junctions have their limitations because they lack accessibility for cleaning, and I would recommend you use them only when you have a rodding point nearby. This could be a roddable type gully, an inspection chamber or simply a rodding access point at the bottom of an above-ground pipe.

Inspection chambers don't have to be large brick-built boxes now. Indeed, since a few deaths have occurred from workman getting into deep manholes without breathing apparatus and being overcome by methane fumes, or becoming trapped, new building laws introduced in 2002 have sought to discourage access to manholes by making them smaller and avoiding step irons being built in. Cleaning can be done from the surface by feeding in rods or high-pressure hoses, without actually getting into the drains yourself. Preformed plastic chambers come in a variety of sizes, beginning with miniature and moving up to deep-access ones.

For sink wastes a trapped gulley is normally used, but because of the high risk of blockages from kitchen sinks, it is worth buying a roddable gulley that has a sealed cleaning point aside the inlet part.

Remember that drainage alterations are controlled under the Building Regulations, which means that they are subject to an application and inspections. Normally, an initial inspection of the pipes and fittings jointed up and lying in the trench bedding is followed after backfill by a drainage test to check it is watertight and OK to use.

Personally, if I'd laid new drains I would want to test them before backfilling the trenches, but you may be keen on digging and refilling trenches for recreation. Drain tests can be done below ground by water pressure, where the end of the pipe run (at an inspection chamber) is sealed off with an expanding plug and the run is filled with water. The water level can then be watched at a convenient point for signs of dropping. After ten minutes or so, if you and the inspector are happy that it hasn't fallen, the test has been passed, but there is no set time for a water test. Sometimes a leaking joint will cause the water to drop fairly quickly, but at other

Close-coupled WC with space-saving connector.

times it may just leak away gradually. Because of this it is worth setting up the test in advance of the inspector's visit and leaving it on for perhaps an hour or more.

Plumbers and drains

I am often amazed at the number of trading plumbers who don't secure joints on their plumbing wastes. Solvent-welded systems actually require the joints to be solvent-welded, and yet you could be forgiven for thinking that some plumbers find this fact a revelation, so many leave them just push-fitted together. I think this might be a habit that has come from site work, where time is tight and taking apart each joint to glue it after it has all been set out is left to a last minute that never comes.

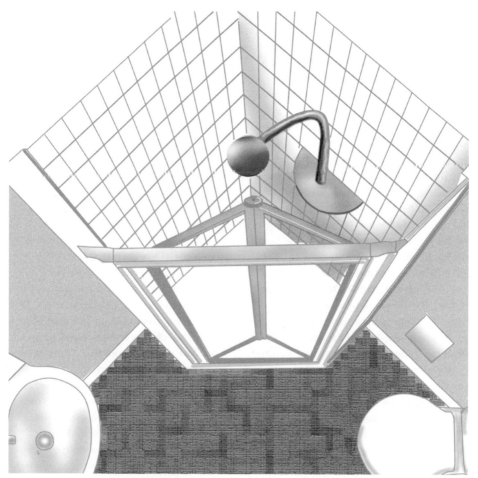

Corner unit fixtures mean en-suites can be added to most bedrooms with nearby drainage.

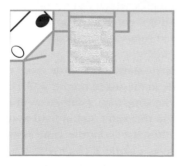

Plan of bedroom with corner en-suite.

Members of the Institute of Plumbers have been given self-certification status under the 2002 Building Regulations to carry out below-ground drainage works as well as plumbing. This is strange, to say the least, because I've yet to meet a plumber who would go anywhere near below-ground drainage – normally they start work at DPC level and only go up from there.

101

Creating extra bathrooms and en-suites

After kitchens come bathrooms, and I have a feeling that bathrooms may take over soon in the vogue stakes. We use them just as often, and it seems like we have only just come alive to the idea that they can be attractive places to visit as well as just places of sanitary convenience. A home with only one bathroom is now considered to be an underdeveloped home, or possibly a flat. If you have daughters, you will know how difficult it is to get access to the bathroom, and to only have the one for the family to share can be torture. I speak from experience.

There are still gaps to be filled in the market. Bathroom light fittings in the year 2003 represent a tiny fraction of the lights available, and creative or attractive ones are as rare as hen's teeth. Vanity units are gradually arriving on the UK market, but the price is exorbitant given that they are flat-packed and mass-produced. France, by comparison, is the vanity unit capital of the world, and a visit to a French DIY store will reveal aisles of variety in design and price. We have all moved into the designer appliance market now, with even our DIY stores selling glass hand basins and multi-function massaging shower cubicles. Bathrooms are now subject to fashion and all the vagaries of it, whereas in the last century they weren't; bathrooms were just places to bathe and exercise your bodily functions.

Given this rise in status, adding an en-suite, converting an old bedroom to a new bathroom or re-modelling your old one is a popular and worthy project. Space is not as demanding as it was, because sanitaryware makers have created corner units for WCs, showers and baths that tuck away into the smallest of rooms.

Showers

Replacing your bath with a shower, or adding a shower to your home is said to save water in itself. Apparently the average shower (this must be the one taken by the average man on the No.10 omnibus that you see appearing in census results) uses 50 l of water less than a bath. But even if water conservation doesn't interest you, showers are by far the most popular in our busy modern lives, where it seems we scarcely have time to get wet.

Shower choice has changed a bit from just mixer or electric. A mixer needs a hot water supply pipe along with a cold one, but at the expense of pressure. It is possible to add pressure with a shower pump, but only from a gravity-fed system. Be warned that pumps can be noisy – I would look to insulating them from whatever you fix them down to. Pumps can't be used with combis, which can't produce hot water quick enough to supply a pumped shower, even those with higher flow rates.

Electric showers are little more than electric kettles fixed on the wall. They have the same immersion element that heats up the water, and in hard-water areas, they last about the same amount of time as a kettle. If you live in a hard-water area and you want an electric shower, buy a cheap one, because in a year or two you will be replacing it – they are disposable items.

Our choice now includes body-massaging showers, with multiple showerheads positioned at a variety of surprising heights. Because of their nature, they come pre-plumbed to a cubicle and are priced accordingly. On a more basic level, thermostatic showers are ideal for those of us with small children or temporary amnesia. They regulate the temperature of the hot water to a maximum level (preset at 43°C) that prevents us from being scalded. You can sometimes adjust the temperature level prior to installation, and some of the more advanced showers have a digital temperature function that controls delivery to your requirements.

Shower controls have come a long way and would be great if only we could find a way of delivering balanced hot and cold water that isn't so hard as to clog everything up with limescale in a few months. They should give away white vinegar with every sale – if you strip a mixer shower down and use it to clean the piston and shower head frequently, you can keep it running for quite a bit longer.

There are some basic check points that you need to strike off when planning any additional bathroom.

● **Air out**

Check that the position of your new room will have some mechanical fan ventilation, extracting out to the open air. It isn't possible to run the fan through unlimited lengths of ducting – a limit exists with all fans, and it must

A wide variety of soil pipe connections are available to join to existing drainage.

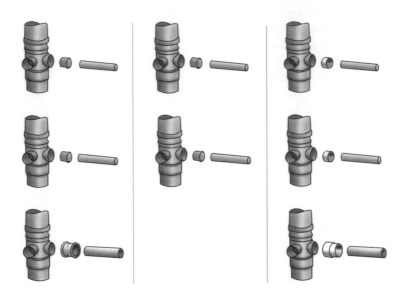

Soil pipe systems can be extended with a variety of fittings.

terminate outside in the fresh air, not in the loft or inside an old chimney or cavity. If you don't have an external wall, ceiling fans can expel out through special roof tiles. The choice with fans always ran along the lines of centrifugal or co-axial, followed by wall-mounted or ceiling mounted and timer or no timer. The truth is they are all undesirable. For my money the in-line fans that let you place the motor in the middle of the duct rather than in the room are the best, because nobody wants to see the thing and certainly nobody wants to

LIMITS FOR WASTE PIPE RUNS AND FITTINGS				
Appliance	Waste pipe size	Max length of waste	Trap size	Standard fall
WC	100 mm	6 m	50 mm	20 mm
Bath	40 mm	3 m	50 mm	20–40 mm
Shower	40 mm	3 m	50 mm	20–40 mm
Basin	32 mm	1.7 m	75 mm	20 mm
Combined	50 mm	4 m	–	20–40 mm

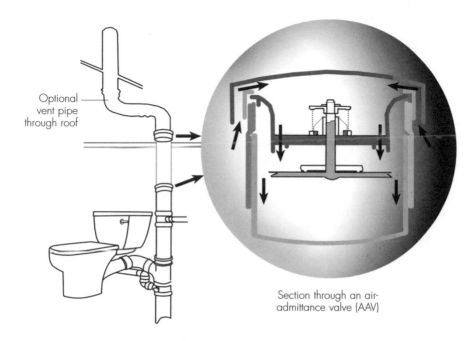

Optional vent pipe through roof

Section through an air-admittance valve (AAV)

Soil pipes can be terminated by AAVs or vent pipes.

hear it. The new low-watt units running off DC voltage burn a lot less electricity and are also quieter.

Switching has also become a bit more advanced, with humidistats now built into many models that switch them on automatically when the humidity reaches a critical level. Start with the in-line fans: if you have a loft void above the ceiling, all you need actually see on the ceiling itself is the duct opening or the duct opening with a low-voltage halogen lamp in the middle of it – and see if you can find one with a humidistat instead of a light switch connection. With the motor in the roof void you have the added

benefit of sound insulation from the ceiling and loft insulation above, but they are fairly quiet to begin with.

● **Air in**
Check that you have some inlet ventilation – a window is nice, but not entirely necessary so long as you have a decent gap under the door or a duct vent to draw in some air.

● **Water in**
Check that your water pipes can serve the new appliances. Usually they travel through floor or roof voids. Plan a path for your hot and cold water supply from its nearest existing position. Plastic

pipes can make the task easier, as they bend around corners where copper would have to be cut and jointed.

● Water out

Check that your foul drainage system can be extended to serve the new appliances. This does actually take some checking too, because waste pipes of any diameter can only run so far unvented. Beyond these limits the pipes can be vented by air admittance valves that draw air in when needed. Conventional drainage works by gravity, and minimum falls on the pipes are needed to keep it that way. If you don't have these minimum falls available, you may have to look at a fully pumped system that runs on electricity. These products have been around for a few decades now, but I've yet to meet anyone who likes them. As a last resort they do the job, but they are a last resort and only when you have a conventional gravity system to accompany them. Nobody wants to be caught short in a power cut.

The fall on waste pipes of 32–50 mm diameter should be between 19 mm and 90 mm per 1 m run. Outside these limits, problems may occur.

With 100 mm pipes for WC pans, the fall should be at the lower gradient of 19 mm per 1 m for a single WC, but if you have long runs of waste and more than one pan connected, you could reduce this to 9 mm per metre.

Improving loft spaces for storage

For most of us, storage space in our homes is sadly lacking, and there are so many things that get used only once or twice a year – Christmas decorations, luggage, the car roof rack, things that you couldn't possible throw out, like your college notes or Cycling Proficiency Certificate, but things that, equally, you couldn't possibly keep in the home. Lofts were seemingly made for these things. Although once again, actually they weren't. Attics have always been up there: in Roman architecture they were the storey or low wall beneath the ornamental façade at the top of a building, but soon became the roof space at this elevation.

Attics have never been pleasant places to visit; in the past, the absence of any roofing felt made them draughty, and now with felt and insulation, the inclusion of roof vents does the same. Combine this with the depth of insulation we now employ above our ceilings, and the attic seems like an inaccessible place. It needn't be.

Upgrading the insulation

Loft insulation has for years conjured up an image of irritating yellow glassfibre quilt with particles you can choke on whenever you dare raise the loft hatch door. It served a purpose and still does, but the thickness of the wretched stuff we now need to meet our energy standards has made it a difficult material to live with. Typically, a 100 mm layer is needed between the ceiling joists, and then a second 150 mm thick layer is needed over the top of that in the opposite direction, covering the joists. Why? Because the standard U value we aim for now is no higher than 0.18 w/m sq k, and the cold-bridging of heat through the timber joists means they must be covered to achieve this.

Insulation like this makes it impossible to traverse the loft without putting your foot through the ceiling, let alone to store much, but there are modern insulation materials that are much thinner and able to achieve the same high levels of insulation without the mess and inconvenience of glassfibre: multi-reflective foil laminates and rigid polyurethane boards. The former can be dressed over the joists, but at only 25 mm thick, it can be left to sag between them and be boarded over with floor sheet boards, which can be installed in 100 mm thick sheets between the joists to achieve a similar level without needing to cover the joists at all. If you were to raise the flooring sheets on bearers to spread the load, you could achieve 150 mm polyurethane foam board insulation in two 75 mm thick layers.

Ceiling joist decking

Decking on ceiling joists is comfortably achieved when it can be screwed down direct to the joist tops, but if you have recessed ceiling spotlights, they should be protected by raised platforms that leave plenty of ventilation space above the lamp. These lamps can get hot, and wrapping them in insulation will help to create the conditions for an electrical overload or a fire.

Decking boards should be lapped or staggered to avoid a continuous joint, and screw-fixing is better than nailing. With tongue-and-groove joints that can also be glued, the decked area of your loft can be smoothly finished to allow

boxes to be slid and moved about. I use wheeled plastic storage boxes in mine, because they are so easy to push across to the hatch for emptying.

How much weight can be stored in the attic?

How much you can store up there safely will vary from loft to loft, but it's worth remembering that trussed rafters were only designed to cope with access for maintenance and repair and not for storage. The design load used for this is 0.5 kn per square metre, which is exactly a quarter of the load allowance used for a house floor. Imagine the kind of weight your furniture represents in your bedrooms, for example, and halve it twice, and you have some idea of what your loft was designed to take. Conventional cut-and-pitched roofs may fare better, depending on the span of the joists.

It isn't uncommon for light storage in attics to impose a loading of up to 1 or even 1.5 kn per square metre of decking, so you would be well advised to check the adequacy of your ceiling before you start to load.

Full water tanks are around a quarter of a tonne in weight, and these are dealt with in attics by spreading the weight on bearers across several joists. Bearers are timber joists running perpendicular across the ceiling joist, with a decking material on top to create the tank stand. If you want to increase the storage load in part of your loft, you can look to using a similar construction with bearers across at least five joists. It will also create extra depth for insulation beneath the bearers.

CHAPTER 6

Structural Repairs

Subsidence or settlement?

Subsidence is on the increase, or at least insurance claims for subsidence are.

But what exactly is subsidence, what are its causes and solutions, and how is it different to settlement? In 1984 the Insurance Ombudsman had to answer some of these questions and make some definitions in order to regulate fairly over claims. It was defined that subsidence is something that happens to the ground, in that it is the soil beneath a property that causes it to move, whether it be the compression of peat, the consolidation of made-up ground or the shrinkage of clay – it is the ground that causes the failure.

Settlement, on the other hand, is something that happens as a result of the building and its weight and design.

Insurance claims

Something that isn't always appreciated is that usually for an insurance claim to be successful, it must be subsidence of the site that has caused the cracks and damage to the home, and not settlement. The latter could have been caused by floor joists or beams, for example, that are bearing an unacceptable weight on walls – in other words, design or workmanship failure. Some degree of settlement occurs in the first few years of a building's life, and the subsoil beneath it also suffers from settlement once it is built on, before entering a period of consolidation. If your home has been poorly built –

Cracks can arise from either subsidence or settlement.

Tree roots

Leaking drains

Excavations

Differential ground movement

Slope instability

Heavy traffic

Subsidence can be caused by a variety of reasons.

Changes in soil conditions

Weak ground

perhaps the foundations were too narrow or the concrete too weak – then settlement can be excessive and at times result in a structural failure, but this doesn't make it subsidence.

All new homes undergo a drying-out period once the owners have moved in and switched the heating on, which results in the property settling down. Shrinkage cracks occur, and although there are new home warranties in place that cover this eventuality in the extreme, your basic buildings insurance will usually exclude it on the grounds that it is bound to happen. Things that are bound to happen are rarely insurable – the whole point of insurance is that there must be an element of 'surprise' to a claim. Even subsidence due to coastal erosion can be difficult to insure against, since given the relentless actions of time and weather, it is bound to happen.

The site as enclosed by the boundary of your property is covered, so it can also be part of the claim if subsidence has damaged fences, patios and paths

and their repair is included with the house. If, on the other hand, the house hasn't been touched but the garden fence is wrecked, a claim for the fence or patio alone is likely to be an unsuccessful one.

Trees and subsidence

So what are the main causes of valid subsidence claims? In the UK 80 per cent of all claims in London and the Southeast are caused by trees desiccating the ground, which in this part of the world is clay. It is thought that between 7 and 10 per cent of homes are near trees, and I fully appreciate just how amenable it is to live in their company. You are always in touch with the seasons and nature with trees around you, and undoubtedly they can make properties more desirable. Pollutants and carbon dioxide are removed from the air, cleaning up your environment, and a large mature tree can take out more than 70 times the pollution than a smaller one. In London there are thought to be around

London clay

Kimmeridge clay, Oxford clay

Lower Lias clay

Gault clay

Weald clay

Mercia mudstone (Keuper marl)

Limit of main areas of glacial deposits

Geological variation of clay soil.

1,400,000 street trees already, but the Highways Agency has suggested that more trees should be planted along the roadsides of Britain to reduce pollution.

Alas, there is a price to pay for living close to trees. A big mature tree like an English oak will lose hundreds of gallons of water from its leaves on a hot day, water that has to be replaced if the tree is to live – and the roots that spread out in search of this water can desiccate a clay soil for up to 30 m or more from the trunk itself. Clay soil behaves particularly badly when sucked dry: it dramatically shrinks in volume, leaving any building sitting on it to subside. Ironically, hard clay soils are worse than soft clay soils when affected by trees, because the tree must work harder to suck the water out, a job that it can do with extraordinary strength. It has been conservatively calculated that a pressure of 300–400 kn per square metre can be exerted on the soil by tree roots doing this – that is three to four times greater than the pressure exerted by the weight of an average house.

It may even be worse in stiff clays such as those found beneath London, where suction pressures could be up to 800 kn per square metre. The combination of trees and buildings can be an unhappy one. For the tree's part it is merely trying to survive in soil so sticky that oxygen exists only in 300 mm or so, and to do this its roots must radiate out near the surface, rather than sink down deep. About half of all tree species have feeding roots consisting of fine matted hairs within 1 m of ground level. In spite of this they are capable of extracting water from the ground at depths of up to 6 or 7 m below.

Of course some trees are thirstier than others; poplars, oaks and willows are among those with the highest water demands, and consequently represent the biggest threats to our homes. Poplars are well adapted to urban life, and willows have no control over their stomata and consequently their rate of transporation, but all of them are only a problem in clay.

In the North of England, a clay-free zone, almost half of all subsidence claims result from leaking drains. Old pipes buried beneath the ground may leak for years undetected, but slowly they soften the ground close to the home's foundations and eventually cause them to subside.

Mining operations, whether they are active or long-abandoned, can cause subsidence too, and indeed published information relating to the position of mine shafts has caused considerable property blight – even where subsidence has not occurred.

Underpinning

Only 15 per cent of insurance claims result in underpinning. This can be a drastic measure and a costly one. In drought years such as 1976, when claims reached £200,000,000, and 1991, when they hit £600,000,000, things reach epidemic proportions.

Underpinning means excavating out the ground beneath the foundations to a depth where the soil will be stable and not suffer from seasonal changes or the effects of trees. Since the whole property cannot be underpinned in one go, it has to be divided up into sections of perhaps 1 m long, which are dug out in a sequence; each one is concreted and dry-packed with a lean mix to the underside of the existing foundation, propping it up until eventually the whole of the scheme is complete. Because only small lengths of foundation can be underpinned at any one time and the vast majority of the digging must be done by hand, the job is time-consuming and expensive. Even so, the insurance industry maintains that the most expensive element is the internal redecoration of the property!

Underpinning and insurance

An excess is usually placed on a buildings policy of £500–1000 to dissuade homeowners from making minor claims. In extreme cases, the residents may have to move out for the work to be carried out, as the property is rendered uninhabitable for the duration of the work.

Some conflicts have arisen in the past where home owners have changed insurers around the time of subsidence. The Insurance Ombudsman has given a ruling for such eventualities – where the claim is made within eight weeks of the change in insurers, the previous insurer must deal with it; if it is made within one year of the change, the costs are split equally 50/50, but if it is later than one year since the changeover, the current policy will apply.

The first problem that you are likely to encounter is the time factor. Since first noticing cracks in your walls and suspecting subsidence, your building insurer may wish to appoint a crack specialist to observe the property over a full year. In doing so, they may see whether the cracks close up in the winter and open in the summer, suggesting seasonal movement of the soil. This may mean that they will choose not to do anything about it unless the movement is very severe, indicating that the problem is not getting worse.

Even if underpinning is found to be necessary, the whole house may not be done; it is more likely that the insurers will only pay out for a partial underpinning scheme for the section where damage has occurred. In this situation, you may find that in the future the newly founded part of the house will have become stationary but the older part is still moving, giving rise to further cracks. This is known as differential settlement. Ongoing differential settlement can mean that several claims will be made over a period of years for partial underpinning schemes, until eventually the entire house is underpinned.

The bit of your home that subsides is the bit that gets underpinned and repaired. Given this risk of differential settlement and future cracking, you would think it would cause insurers at least to blink. They appear not to acknowledge this problem and quite happily continue to receive claims and underpin parts of homes as and when failures occur. Insurance doesn't deal with prevention – only cure, you just have to keep reminding yourself.

The words 'subsidence' and 'underpinning' can be a worry, raising concerns of disruption and blight. But these events need not affect the future sale of the property. Clearly a home that has been underpinned entirely is likely to be a much stronger and robust home for it, its saleability should be enhanced. Partially underpinned homes, or minor works that arrest movement by drain repairs, for example, are best protected by continued insurance. You can also purchase a warranty from the specialist contractor that guarantees their work. Expect to get cover for at least 20 years – but only for the work that has been done – and in this light the warranty shouldn't be used in lieu of maintained cover with your existing insurers, who

5

Crack with width in millimetres

 4

Surface step in millimetres – arrow flight indicates depressed side of crack

Crack considerably wider at the top than the bottom

Crack with shear in directions shown

Crack showing signs of compression

Crack the other side of the wall

Labelling cracks on plans.

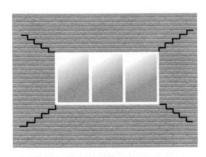

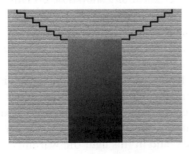

Cracks tend to form around openings where stress is focused.

will have a full record of what has been done to the property.

Identifying cracks

Cracks are like spiders – most of us don't like them, whatever their size; maybe we tolerate the smaller ones, annoying though they are, but big ones, absolutely not.

Minor cracks to our plastering indoors are annoying, but with filler and paint we can deal with them: after all, they are usually only caused by the heating and drying out of wood and plaster. So when do cracks become portents of much worse?

Like wind speeds and earthquakes, cracks are measured on a scale, a simple 0–5 table designed by the Building Research Establishment, with the tiniest hairline fractures at one end and gorges at the other.

As you can see opposite, cracks up to 5 mm wide, in spite of being unsightly décorwise, are not considered to be of any structural importance. But it isn't just the width of cracks that needs observing; their position and shape should always be recorded. Arrays of cracks can occur diagonally across a wall, wider at the top than the bottom, implying that part of the building is subsiding, with the foundations moving down in this area.

Features of subsidence cracks

● Usually they are diagonal across a wall

● Usually they taper in width, wider at one end than the other

CATEGORY OF DAMAGE	DESCRIPTION OF CRACKING AND DAMAGE	ACTION REQUIRED
0	Hairline cracks around 0.1 mm wide	None
1	Fine cracks up to 1 mm wide	Fill during decoration
2	Cracks 1–5 mm wide	Repointing may be needed externally. Inside covering with linings etc.
3	Cracks 5–15 mm wide or several 3 mm wide or more; sticking doors and windows	Opening up cracks and re-stitching brickwork, replacing bricks if cracked; partial underpinning of foundations may be needed
4	Cracks 15–25 mm wide, distorted window and door frames	Underpinning. Sections of wall to be rebuilt
5	Cracks more than 25 mm, walls leaning, danger of collapse	Underpinning and rebuilding of walls, or total demolition and rebuild

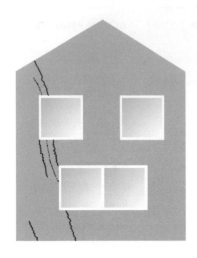

Typical pattern of subsidence cracking.

- Cracks on the outside have corresponding cracks inside. Subsidence means that both faces of the wall crack, not just one, although they don't always line up in the same place

- Cracks caused by the action of tree roots on the soil are usually wider at the top, as the building is effectively tilted towards the tree

Monitoring cracks

Your insurers may decide to employ a crack monitoring specialist or engineer to monitor the cracks over a year or 18 months, observing any changes of the rate of subsidence from season to season. There are a number of ways they can do this: overlapping plastic plates with vernier scales can be screw-fixed to the wall over the crack, and will measure movement in two dimensions. Alternatively, metal studs can be driven into the wall, floor or ground, and callipers can be used to measure the distance between these fixed points

- The widest end of the crack is always at the free end, such as the corner or top of the wall, or the edge of a door or window opening

- Usually they move around window and door openings, continuing on the other side

No action needed.

Action needed.

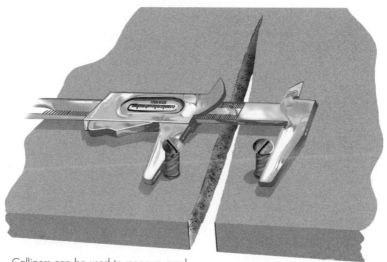

Callipers can be used to measure crack widths between fixed studs

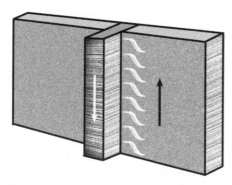

Movement can occur in more than one direction

Subsidence cracks are often wider at the top

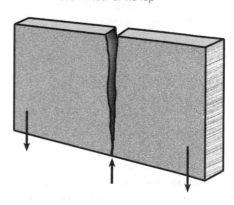

Monitoring crack movement.

CHAIN OF EVENTS

Cracks seen

Notify insurers and register a claim

Insurers appoint a structural engineer or crack monitoring expert

Is crack damage unacceptable and in need of structural treatment?

Yes	No
Monitoring and Investigation of damage	Advice on cause and any repairs or prevention needed
Underpin foundations and repair floors, leaking drains, etc.	
Repair walls	
Redecorate	

periodically. Glass 'tell-tale' strips can be fixed across the crack – these break when movement occurs – but all this tells you is that the subsidence is still active, not what to do.

Cracks due to thermal movement

Walls can expand through solar heating in the summer or even saturation in the winter, but often the compressive stress isn't enough to crush the wall. Instead, it breaks the frictional resistance with the damp-proof course and moves along it. Alas, when it later cools down or dries out and shrinks, the resulting

tensile stress is often less than its compressive counterpart and lower than the frictional resistance of the DPC – meaning the wall cracks. Given time, the crack fills up with debris and gets gradually wider each year, until it eventually becomes a problem waiting to be addressed.

I've read that a tiny movement of 0.5 mm in a 3 m long wall can produce a bulge in the wall of up to 25 mm out of plane. This apparently is because the deformation occurs at right angles to the movement and force that created it. So what is the solution to this kind of thermal movement?

Expansion joints can be cut into overly long walls to reduce the brickwork into panels that can expand without causing any damage. They are normally cut with a circular 'skill' saw, which with the right blade thickness can carve out a slot for an expansion material to be inserted and pointed over with silicone mastic. Expansion-board strips in brick widths are a fibreboard-type material that absorbs the movement by compression. Brown mastic is usually chosen for brickwork since at least it drops in on the same colour range; white just doesn't look right unless you have rendered walls painted white.

Cracks in concrete floors

It isn't just walls that suffer from subsidence – ground floors crack as well, and in the past this exceeded the number of subsidence claims over foundations. The usual reason for floors cracking comes from settlement of the hardcore on which they were formed. There are tight controls in place today governing the type and quality of the hardcore material used beneath floor slabs, because substandard work here always comes back to the surface. Many homes have had their floors built over a rubble infill or poorly compacted hardcore, and over time this has gradually consolidated, robbing the floor slab of support.

Usually it is enough to break up the concrete floor, dig out the fill and do the job again properly with approved materials and workmanship, but if the depth of fill exceeds 600 mm, an alternative may be necessary. A reinforced suspended slab can be formed from the caps of mini-piles driven into the ground beneath the floor – imagine a table with many legs below ground. These mini-piles can be bashed in to depths of up to several metres if need be, in search of good load-bearing conditions, making them ideal for underpinning slabs on filled ground sites. If your hardcore depth is somewhere between 600 mm and 1 m, it may prove more economical to use concrete in layers with hardcore to make up the extra fill.

The best hardcore materials are those that once compacted into place will never consolidate, like stone. Indeed, they need very little compaction at all, just enough to shuffle them about like a bag of marbles until they have found their position of minimum voids. Other materials, like crushed concrete fines and Type 1 sub-base, need to be compacted by mechanical plate compactors that whack them down to a billiard-table finish.

Slabs don't just fail by settlement; they can be lifted by unstable fill material. Colliery shale has a reputation for this, because in its burnt form it is saturated with soluble sulphates that attack the concrete slab, causing it to arch up and crack. This movement can also cause the walls to bulge out, but if they haven't been damaged the slab and its fill can be broken up and removed. Don't allow your builders to re-use the broken-up concrete slab as hardcore for the new one, since it will be contaminated by sulphates wanting to repeat the event.

Finding the cause of subsidence

Two main culprits stand behind the smoking gun when it comes to subsidence: drains and trees. There are others, but let's take a look at these two villains first.

Drains

Drains have a habit of leaking when they get old; they may even become broken or holed, and in time the leaking water will saturate the ground permanently. How long it takes is anyone's guess, and depends in part on the subsoil type, but permanently saturated ground beneath your foundations is not a good thing to have, and subsidence is inevitable. Sandy soils, alluvials and gravels are prone to water erosion, and some rocks like limestone and chalk are susceptible to the formation of swallet holes – pockets formed below ground by the erosion of soil and rock – and even caverns formed by water erosion. Some soils will just collapse with the loss of volume after going through a traumatic rearrangement of their particles. What could once have been fixed in a few hours by replacing a broken section of drain pipe will now take weeks and incur great expense.

Leaking drains are the invisible menace. Drainage can be tested to check if it is watertight, and CCTV surveys can be carried out to locate the point of leakage. Often where the soil vent pipe comes down or where a gully occurs, the drain directly beneath it at this connection is broken and the water is seeping into the ground directly

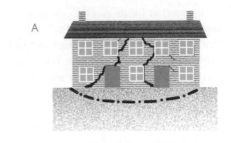

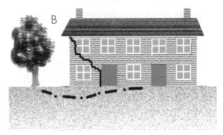

Cracking pattern of subsidence (A and B) and heave (C).

beside the foundations. Foul water accelerates the soil erosion with biological action.

If you're buying a property with old cracks that have been described as historic or were patched up years ago, beware. They are often dismissed because of their age as of no concern, but cracks can reappear in time, and an investigation may well reveal a broken drain or water pipe that has been left to carry on leaking.

Cracks occur nearest to trees where root action is the cause.

Trees

Trees have no respect for boundaries: branches and roots travel freely, and you may not have the luxury of deciding what to do with an offending tree. You should seek recompense through the courts for any damage caused by a neighbouring tree – courts are able to award an injunction against the tree's owner, requiring them to prevent its trespass any further. The problem is, of course, in considering liability: the courts must decide whether the tree owner was negligent and could have reasonably foreseen and prevented the problems it has caused you, and this is where most claims run aground. It obviously helps if your soil is clay and the tree was planted near your home after it was built.

Roots and branches can be cut back where they cross a boundary, but cutting roots that are larger than 50 mm in diameter can destabilise a tree, and is

121

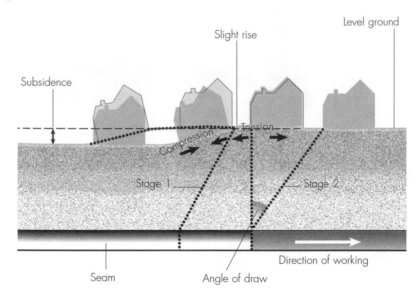

Longwall mining and the effects of subsidence wave.

thus considered to be a bad idea. The tree owner can claim against you if the tree dies or falls.

Assuming the offending tree or trees are on your land and are known to be younger than your home (and the damage isn't too severe), removing them can be part of the solution. The problem comes when the tree is older or of unknown age, because then the effects of the clay swelling, or heaving as the industry calls it, can be just as damaging to your home after the tree has been removed. Because of these issues, underpinning is the preferred option, to a depth that more or less guarantees that the ground beneath the new foundations can't be troubled in the future.

Conventional underpinning of foundations is carried out by digging and concreting small sections of foundation beneath the existing ones; and where trees in clay are present, this can sometimes mean to a depth of several metres – the deepest underpinning trenches I've seen have been 5.5–6 m deep. Hand-digging at these depths opens up issues of health and safety for the groundworkers. Pad and beam underpinning is a better solution if these depths are anticipated, since shallow reinforced ground beams can be formed (in sections) between deep-fill concrete pad foundations formed at the corners.

Root barriers

When I mentioned about taking steps to prevent tree root growth doing more damage, what I meant was not cutting them or killing them off, but installing

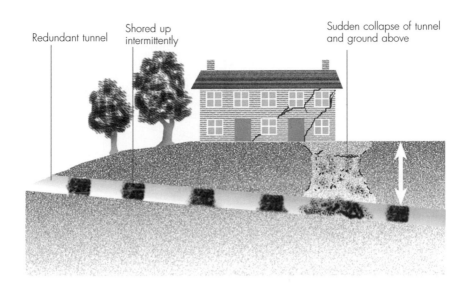

Underground works can give rise to sudden collapse.

root barriers to restrict their spread. Usually a narrow trench, no more than 300 mm wide, is dug and concreted to a depth of several metres that will guard against the roots passing under. It's important that the barrier is continuous and up to ground level, if not slightly above it for the same reason. If it's lined with polythene on the home side, any heave will slide up it, rather than damage it. Root barriers don't have to be concrete; they can be any materials that will resist roots and won't degrade in the ground.

Mining and underground work

Subsidence due to underground works like mining or tunnelling happens from time to time. When it does it usually makes the news because a football pitch-sized hole in the ground has opened up overnight drawing attention to itself in the way that holes of this size do. The last one I saw occurred when a railway tunnel gave way close to new homes; thankfully it stopped at swallowing the road, but the homes were close enough to be in trouble all the same. Or was it the World War One tunnels honed from the chalk as practice for the Royal Engineers that collapsed after 80 years with the same effect? There are towns in this country that are labyrinthed by tunnels and underground workings dug in wartime.

The technique of longwall mining for coal can cause a subsidence wave that damages homes as the wave passes beneath. Once it has gone, the building is left stable, but sometimes properties on the edge of the subsidence zone can

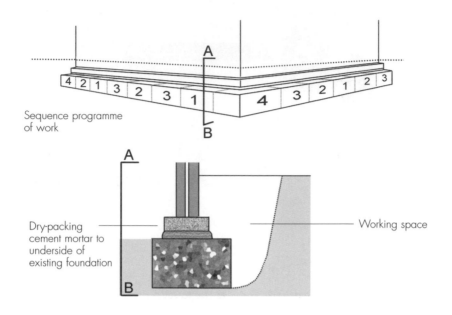

Sequence programme of work

Dry-packing cement mortar to underside of existing foundation

Working space

Traditional underpinning.

be left sitting on differing levels, causing subsidence cracks. The zone affected within a given distance of mine shafts has been prone to change in the past, blighting properties that had been purchased outside it and then found themselves in it, regardless of whether they had suffered any subsidence. It isn't always history's fault either – the Austrian tunnelling technique was much admired until they tried it at Heathrow Airport and undermined the car park.

Traditional underpinning

Traditional underpinning is a process of labour. Its tenet is one piece at a time, dividing up the foundation to be underpinned into sections or bays typically 1 m long. The bays are numbered individually, but the numbering belies the sequence in which they are each to be dug out and concreted, and hence is not consecutive. Instead it jumps bays so that no two sections are dug out or recently underpinned at one time, as the effect of doing this could weaken your home. Eventually, the underpinned bays all join together to form the completed work of underpinning.

Engineers like to see the bays joined or bonded together, and to this end steel bars are sometimes hammered halfway into the earth end of the

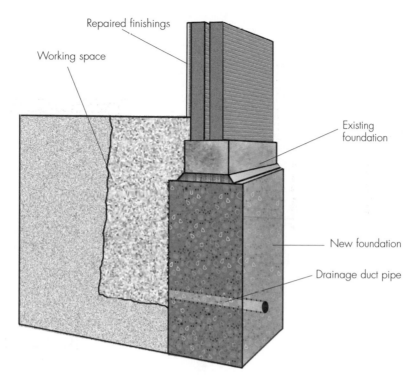

Underpinning.

trenches so they later become cast into the concrete. An alternative to this is to cut teeth into the earth sides with a spade, or to temporarily shutter them with corrugated boarding, thus creating ends that interlock with each other. Be warned, though, that opinion is varied and there are engineers who consider anything of that ilk to be a complete waste of time. If you would like to refer to it, the British Standard for underpinning is BS:8004.

To an independent observer the one thing that is noticeable about underpinning work is that somebody else must be paying for it. Insurance is a wonderful thing when it generates such

quality and thoroughness, but it has a downside in that it doesn't deal in prevention – only cure.

Pile and beam underpinning

Few home-owners experience the trauma of deep-pile underpinning, and in most cases it wouldn't be possible to get the equipment needed that close to the property. Short-piling is a different matter. The rigs are small and can even be set up in your front room if you have to support a new lounge floor on piles. They come in a few different forms, but the principal types are steel-cased driven piles and precast driven piles. Both are gradually thumped into the

125

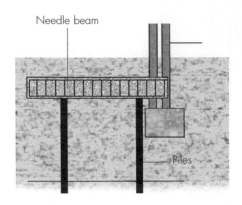

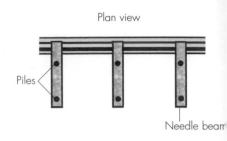

Plan view

Reinforced concrete needle beam underpinning

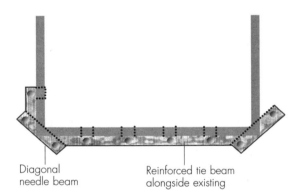

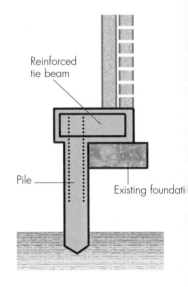

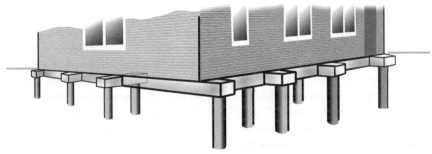

Pile and beam underpinning.

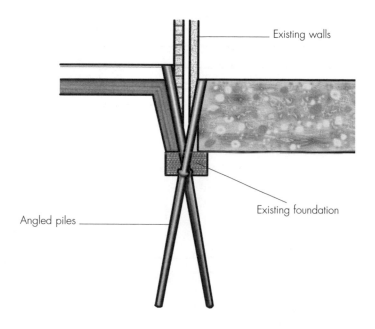

Existing walls

Angled piles

Existing foundation

Angle pile underpinning.

ground to a given resistance that spells out good ground, whether this be at 2 or 7 m deep. The process is slow, since with each thump the pile is only driven in a matter of a few centimetres.

Once all the piles are in place, the ground beams can be set up to bear on them. Traditionally, ground beams are reinforced cages of steel bars formed inside plywood boxing known as formwork. It's usually the case that these beams go beneath the wall but over the existing foundation, which technically would be overpinning rather than underpinning, but I am in danger of confusing us both if I start using that

term. The formwork is the mould for the concrete to be poured in. As with conventional underpinning, ground beams have to be constructed in bays.

Needle beams achieve the same result and are no different in construction, but instead of running along beneath the wall continuously, they run at right angles to it in short lengths. If the floor is not damaged inside and you want to keep it that way, they can be cantilevered off a pair of piles sunk outside. In this way the pile closest to the wall acts under compression and the other one under tension. The wall is supported –

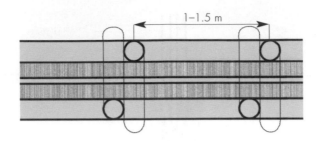

Plan view of angled piles.

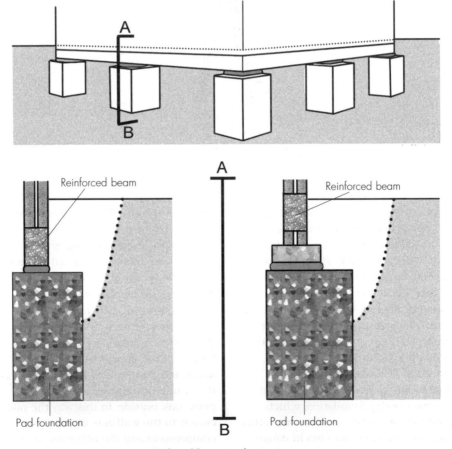

Pad and beam underpinning.

underpinned – by needle beams placed at every 1 m or so apart. It might not sound enough, but brickwork walls can usually arch over distances like this, and needle supports are effective. Essentially it's a similar technique to using needle beams to support chimneys.

Angled pile underpinning

Piles can be in driven directly at angles through holes drilled in the original foundation, and can be employed without the use of ground beams to support the foundation. Because of this, it's a quicker process but a specialist one that is not suited for all conditions.

Injection underpinning

This is specialist stuff again. You know that expanding foam stuff you buy in cans, which fills the holes you squirt it into and then keeps expanding out of it until you wonder if it won't engulf the room. Imagine that being injected via an extra-long tube into the ground beneath your subsiding foundations. The resin expands so enthusiastically that it fills any voids in the soil and lifts the failing foundation. It can be used for up to 3 m beneath the foundations, and expands to 30 times its liquid form exerting pressures around 50 tonnes per square metre on the soil and compressing it against further movement.

I have no idea what the environmental effects of pumping rigid polyurethane foam into the ground are, but I suspect that they can't be good.

Mini-pile floor underpinning

When ground floors have cracked and dropped away, the cause is often down

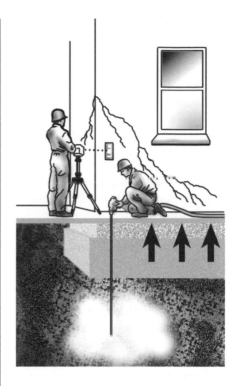

Polyurethane resin injection underpinning.

to bad workmanship or materials in the sub-base construction. What is usually employed in these cases is a man with a pneumatic hammer point, and several more with shovels and wheelbarrows. The slab is busted up and the loose fill beneath dug out so that a new floor can be properly constructed on a new and sound sub-base – messy but effective.

On the other hand, if subsidence is the cause and the fault lies with the subsoil beneath the slab dropping away, then mini-piling can be carried out to underpin the floor slab like legs on a table. Mini piles are installed by mini-piling rigs, little room-sized tripod-mounted machines than can occupy your lounge comfortably – they are not so discreet that you can carry on watching TV while they go in, however. The piles are either augured or driven into the ground to a depth where they meet solid ground. There is a limit on how deep they can be used to avoid buckling, which relates to about 75 times their diameter, which can be anywhere between 65 mm (5 m maximum depth) and 300 mm (22.5 m maximum depth).

The first stage of the floor underpinning process involves holes being drilled in the slab about 1m apart, and grouting being injected into any voids or spaces detected in the fill material beneath. Make sure that your contractors have checked that the grouting hasn't found its way into your cavity walls, which can lead to damp problems later. The piles themselves are placed at no more than 1.5 m apart and no further in from the edges of the floor slab than 300 mm. If you have any internal partition walls built off the slab, then you can expect to see additional piles nearby supporting them, likewise to either side of the cracks in the floor. Driven piles can be steel-cased or precast concrete, and are thumped into the ground in sections with mind-numbing repetition by a compressed air-powered hammer.

Because the process is internal and services like water, drains, gas or electric may be buried under or in the floor, your piling operation should be properly supervised and not left to the workmen operating the machinery. A reputable piling company should provide a site

Boroscope survey of wall ties.

engineer to supervise the job, which may only take two or three days.

Wall repairs
Crack repairs
After the underpinning work has been completed comes the task of repairing the cracks, partly in the name of structural repair but also for weather resistance. Most people prefer to see damaged bricks chopped out and identical replacements bedded in, all freshly pointed with the same mortar mix as the original – in other words, invisible stitching. If underpinning wasn't decreed necessary and the task at hand is to simply repair the cracks, it is worth considering some specialist reinforcing products.

Mortar joint reinforcement often comes in two distinct forms: twisted steel bars that look a lot like drill bits,

Drilling for remedial wall tie fixings.

and expanded metal laths. Both seek to strengthen the masonry and prevent it cracking again. Given a nice horizontal crack running through a bed joint, I can see how raking it out, reinforcing it and repointing it can make a better job, but cross-stitching repair solutions for vertical cracks are less impressive. These cracks sometimes remain in place and are simply filled with a weatherproof silicone filler, functionally adequate but somewhat lacking cosmetically; you might just as well paint a yellow circle around them. Given the choice I would opt for replacement matching bricks and a freshly plastered wall inside, that will underline the fact that I am living in a stronger and better home.

Cavity wall tie failure

The two skins of cavity walls have traditionally been bonded together with metal wall ties. Without them, the individual skins would not be strong enough to act as an external wall. So critical are they to the stability of the cavity wall, that once they have rusted and broken, collapse is almost inevitable – often occurring with the next high winds. I've had the 'privilege' of scrambling over the outer skin of a brick wall that had collapsed suddenly and dramatically into a heap of rubble with a TV aerial. Whether it was the sudden loss of the night's viewing or the brief thunder of the collapse that drew the owner's attention I wasn't sure, but I can testify that cavity wall failure can occur spontaneously. As the inner skin that carries the floor or roof usually stays put, the danger is more acute to people outside the home than inside it.

Now, in enlightened times, wall tie metal with a galvanised coating or stainless steel is used to extend the life of the product, but to begin with it seems the thickness of the coating was too minimal to eliminate the threat of corrosion entirely. The standards for coating were increased in 1986.

Even so it takes time for wall ties to rust and fail, in fact decades of time and exposure to the damp, and so older homes built with facing bricks exposed to the elements are at the greatest risk. The first metal ties were used as far back as the late 19th century, and we have no shortage of century-old homes in Britain built this way. A survey of English houses in 1986 reported the figure to be around 12,000,000, of which about 1,000,000 needed repairs of some sort.

Spotting wall tie failure

Wall tie failure can manifest itself in the form of bulging walls or displaced roof timbers or, with more subtlety, in the form of horizontal cracks. If the wall has been distorted in some way, the only way to repair it may be to rebuild it, but methods of installing new ties to walls are available to arrest the failure before it becomes dangerous.

If you think your home may be suffering by virtue of its age and exposure, even if no cracking has occurred, you can have the ties inspected relatively painlessly. As anyone who has ever been subjected to an endoscopy will tell you, cameras can be fed into some narrow spaces now. In a similar procedure the boroscope camera is fed into the cavity through a drilled hole in the wall and you can see for yourself the state of your internal cavity and its ties. If they are in trouble, remedial ties can be fitted to the wall to prevent it suffering. The job of remedial wall tie treating isn't time-consuming, nor is it that expensive; indeed, the cost of scaffolding the house is often the largest proportion of the sum. Different types of remedial ties are available, but essentially they fall into one of five categories:

- Resin-grouted anchor

- Mechanical expansion

- Friction-fixed

- Combination mechanical expansion/resin grout

- Inflated sock type

Injecting cavity walls

One other method exists of remedially tying the wall together: injecting it with polyurethane foam, essentially the same stuff I mentioned in underpinning: the same hole-filling, stick-to-anything insulating gunk that is fast becoming the building product of the age, along with MDF. Not only does it expand, filling the cavity from its injection points, it grips the inner surfaces of the wall when it sets, bonding them and insulating them all in one – assuming the cavity was clean and free from any insulation to start with. Worth considering? Yes, but also worth considering is what effect this might have on the wall's weather resistance

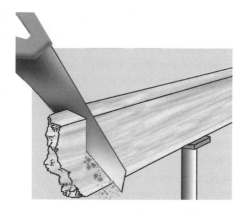

Saw off rotten ends

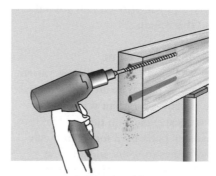

Drill for dowel bars

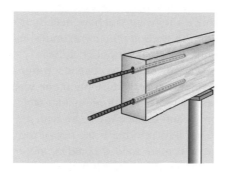

Insert bars with resin bonding

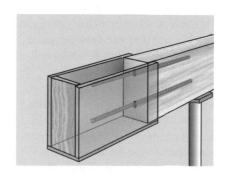

Set formwork

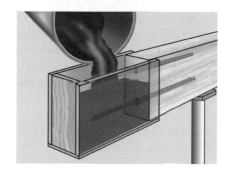

Pour resin timber

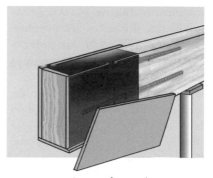

Remove formwork

Resin timber repair.

once removed of the cavity. If the wall has a facing brick outer skin and is exposed to wind-driven rain, I would avoid this option.

Types of cavity wall tie

Even cavity wall construction is varied, and some types of tie are better suited than others to different walls. Mechanical expansion ties are like those expansion bolts used for fixing really heavy things to walls, and are best suited to hard bricks. Having marked out the wall with the tie positions, holes are drilled through and stainless steel ties are inserted before being tightened up. As they are tightened they expand, gripping the masonry. Soft bricks will not enjoy this procedure, so resin-bonded or friction-fix ties are used instead. The names describe how they work, but be aware that the resin is a powerful chemical adhesive that most professionals in the building industry consider to be superior to any other fixing available.

As a preventative measure, wall tie replacement is effective, but you need also to be sure it is necessary. A qualified and independent surveyor can provide you with an investigation and report on the condition of your ties, and hence draw some conclusions about their life expectancy. With a few ties exposed on each elevation of your home, surveyors are able to refer to published sampling methods for gauging the thickness of galvanising. Homes built between 1964 and 1985, when the galvanising treatment was less than it is today, would benefit from such an inspection once every ten years or so.

Timber beam repair

It isn't always easy or economical to replace timber that has rotted or broken, and splicing it with steel plates along the sides is fine only if it isn't on show, so other methods sometimes need to be considered, such as epoxy-resin bonding. A variety of methods with resin bonding are available, depending on the situation, but they all involve inserting bonding rods of a twisted metal nature as dowel bars to strengthen the joint.

In the case of a timber beam in a basement supporting a ground floor above, the beam will have been built into the walls at either end, and over time, with the dampness of the basement walls it has become rotten and is starting to fail. Option one would be to support the floor on adjustable props and replace the beam with a brand new one, but if the rest of the beam is quite solid, it could be more economical to repair it with resin bonding. The beam itself would need to be supported by adjustable props so that the defective end can be sawn off back to the sound wood. Given a drill and some resin, two dowel bars can be bonded halfway into the exposed end of the beam and a shuttering box of waxed and sealed formwork made as a mould to the missing end. Resin is poured in and allowed to cure before the formwork is removed.

If the beam is located in your living space and is perhaps of a sizeable and pleasant appearance, and replacing the end of it can only look right in the same material, the resin can be simply used to bond the dowel bars into the predrilled

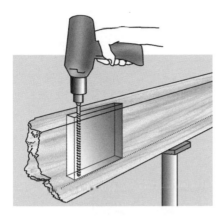

Route a channel

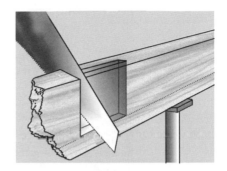

Saw off broken end

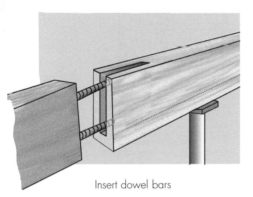

Insert dowel bars

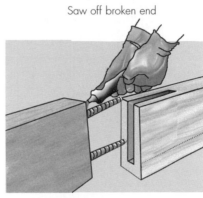

Bond in to new with epoxy resin

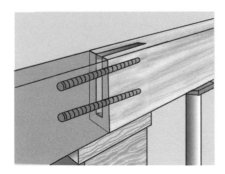

Support jointed beam

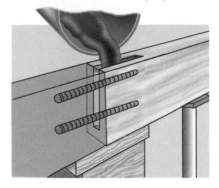

Pour resin timber to channel

Resin-bonded repair of broken timber beam.

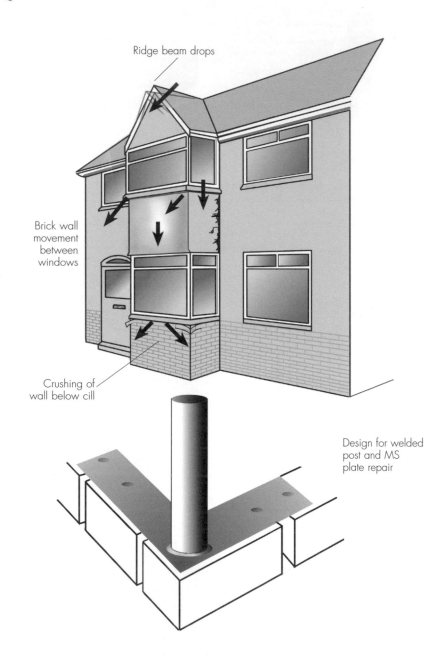

Ridge beam drops

Brick wall movement between windows

Crushing of wall below cill

Design for welded post and MS plate repair

Bay window failure.

holes of the old and new wood. On occasions this can entail some extra work if the quantity of resin needed means the bars have to be set into a hollowed-out channel in the existing beam. Given the liquid state of this stuff when applied and the fact that gravity is never switched off (not even at weekends), the channel can only be routed out from the topside of the beam, so the bars and resin can be dropped and poured in. This places some limitations on its use to joist-supporting beams, where access can be got from above the joists and work carried out in between them. On the plus side, if you can find a nice section of matching timber, at least colourwise (the grain is never going to match), it can be an economical solution as well.

Timber posts can be repaired in a similar way, although it is usually necessary to install vertically inclined dowel bars to resist any lateral force in the joint. The resin itself will take care of the vertical (compressive) load. Resin bonding is something often employed by firms specialising in property repair offering structural design and cost estimating services as well.

Traditional and modern

It's a sign of the times I know, but we're increasingly seeing modern materials being used in combination with traditional methods – scarf joints in oak plates, for example, that are bonded with polyurethane wood adhesive, high-strength stuff that expands slightly to fill any gaps, sets hard in 30 minutes and is 100 per cent water resistant. These glues, sold as thixotropic gels for use in mastic guns or aerosols, are universally employed now for sticking anything except plastic – concrete, masonry, timber, stone, no problem: they seem to permanently bond anything that doesn't have a polished non-absorbent surface.

Bay window failure

Bay windows are a common and popular feature of Victorian and Edwardian homes. In addition to their architectural value, the amount of light they provide within the rooms can often sell the property by itself. Sometimes, however, they can behave less favourably. Bays of this era were often built to two storeys with small gable end roofs cutting into the main roof, the walls themselves being formed from solid one-brick construction and ornate corner posts at the window corners. These timber or cast-iron moulded posts were on sale to builders from merchant's yards and in common use at the time.

Failure of bay windows is normally placed under the heading of settlement rather than subsidence, meaning that the loads on the bay and its construction have made it lean out. The ridgeline of a bay roof may drop towards its gable, tapered cracks (wider at the top) may appear at the abutments with the main wall and the brickwork beneath the windows may be pushed out. Fanlights or casements to the first floor windows may not open properly, and at ground-floor level the window cill itself may be compressed beneath the mullions (posts) of the window frame. All in all, the thing is leaning out away from the house, pitching forwards.

Typical settlement failure like this, however, is not usually covered by insurance: if subsidence was the cause here, stepped cracking would be present and the brickwork and foundations would be dropping out of line. Without these features and the definition that goes with them, a claim on your building insurance may not be successful.

Sometimes the failure has been invoked by the replacement of the windows with plastic ones, because the structural posts at the corners of the old frames have been discarded with the old frames and not replaced. Replacement window companies have a habit of believing that the small metal reinforcing tubes built inside their plastic frames qualify them as loadbearing and able to withstand any weight. Loadbearing windows do not exist, and it is always necessary to have lintels and bearings for those lintels over windows.

Occasionally, it is just time and age that have brought the structure to this state, and lack of maintenance may just have advanced the deterioration. There is no easy cure – structural repairs are needed to arrest the down-and-out movement, and may also include new lintels and posts at the corners secured to spreader plates over the brickwork. The plates will need to be bolted to the walls to restrain them, and the brickwork itself will need to be stitched and tied back into the main walls. In this way a replacement framework of support is introduced to carry the failing one.

If you have noticed that your bay window is starting to move, it is possible to restrain it at an early stage with less expense. A structural engineer will be able to specify a scheme of remedial work for a builder to follow. Ultimately, if left to continue moving, it may become dangerous and may even eventually collapse.

Roof structure repair
Spreading roof syndrome

The triangle is, as we've known for thousands of years, a strong shape. With its corners fixed together, you can push it down as much as you like without fear of it spreading. That's why triangles make such good roofs – but take out one side and replace it with vertical walls, and you court a problem. With nothing to tie back the ends of the rafters the roof shape pushes outwards, spreading. The vertical loads in a roof can be significant, and the angle or pitch of the roof converts some of that downward loading into horizontal force. A 45° roof will split half its loads to vertical and half to horizontal. A 30° pitch will have more horizontal than vertical, and armed with some trigonometry and a wet Sunday afternoon, you can calculate the percentage for yourself.

In modern homes the ceiling joists are our roof ties – when they're fixed to the rafters adequately they resist this horizontal force, nicely completing the triangle. In older buildings where the connections have become broken or the ties damaged or removed, only the walls can save the roof from spreading. Walls have a bad reputation for achieving this; they just aren't thick enough or strong enough at roof plate level to succeed, which is why you see some old buildings sporting metal tie bars. These bars were the traditional method of restraining outward-leaning walls suffering from roof spread. Threaded through to the floor between outside walls, they were finished with nuts that could be tightened over end plates.

In the case of old timber farm buildings, wire hawsers are still used to achieve the same result; they can be wrapped around key members like posts or wall plates and tightened with a turnbuckle to restrain the movement. If you are adopting this method on a timber building that is behaving badly, remember that the aim is to restrain it from further collapse, not to try and pull it back into its original shape. It has taken years, decades and possibly centuries for this movement to occur, and trying to reverse it in the course of an afternoon is not a good idea. Overtightening a hawser or tie bar will cause damage to the structure.

Hawsers need battens to prevent them from cutting into the structural timber, and the end result is not so pretty as to be used for home repairs. In conversion work you must repair tie beams that have broken, and joints and connections so that they work efficiently again and look acceptable.

Repairing truss rafter roofs

Starting with the modern home, by which I mean anything built since the 1960s, you will not be staggered and amazed to learn that trussed rafters can be damaged – yes, those flimsy, thin webs of wood pinned together by thin

metal plates are not immune to failure. The roof plates may be galvanised, but if they were damaged in the fixing by a carpenter thumping 4 in (100 mm) nails through them into the wall plate, time and roof void condensation will inevitably rust them.

While most trusses were designed only to accommodate access for maintenance and repair to the loft, some of us have loaded out our lofts like charity shops. Chipboard loft boards make it easy for use to convert lofts into floors for improved storage, and I've seen wardrobes stocked with clothes and packing cases packed with books, multiplying the dead weight on those ceiling ties beyond what they were designed for. There must be a limit to how much weight they will take before they are damaged.

Repairing trussed rafters is not something you can undertake casually. Ideally, the original manufacturers of the trusses, or another trussed roof manufacturer should be engaged in designing the repair. They will use specialist computer models to analyse the stress in each joint and member individually, and will be able to suggest a way of splicing alongside a break. Plywood or steel plate can be used cut to a shaped gusset, which can be screwed or bolted to either side to act as a splint.

Repairing cut-and-pitched roofs

Traditional cut-and-pitched roofs can suffer damage as well. Particularly vulnerable are the purlins supporting rafters, which become overstressed and

PURLIN SPANS FOR VARIOUS SIZES, GRADES AND SPACINGS

Purlin	C16				Grade	C24		
Size (mm)					Strut spacings (m)			
	1500	2100	2400	2700	1500	2100	2400	2700
50 x 150								
75 x 150	2.00	1.80	–	–	2.10	1.90	1.80	–
50 x 175	2.10	1.95		1.80	–	2.15	1.90	1.85	–
50 x 200	2.40	2.10	2.00	1.85	2.50	2.20	2.10	2.00
50 x 225	2.70	2.35	2.20	2.00	2.80	2.45	2.35	1.90

break. Roofs were invariably formed from 2 x 4 in (50 x 100 mm) timbers until the advent of trusses, and having managed to hang together perfectly well for 50 years or so, they often start to suffer with improved insulation and roof tile replacement. When the houses were built, insulation was thin if not actually unheard of, close boarding over the rafters was sometimes used instead of felt, and the tiles on the roof could well have been lightweight asbestos or natural slate.

As the years have passed the home's more recent residents may have recovered the roof with heavier concrete tiles, and will certainly have added more insulation to the roof. The extra weight on the rafters may have caused them to sag or the purlins to break, and the increased temperature difference between the rooms below and the loft space may have given rise to condensation and damp. Damp timbers begin to rot.

Broken purlins can be repaired with spliced-in timbers scarf-jointed together, and rotten timbers can be replaced with new ones, but ultimately the roof may need strengthening with extra support. An indication of how far purlins can span is given in the table above. Reference to it will help you to recognise whether additional struts should be introduced to reduce the span of your purlins and thus arrest their sagging.

In historic homes, carpenters repairing timbers should be encouraged to carve the date of the repair into the wood along with their initials. It may seem unnecessarily flamboyant, but it will help historians working on the story of the building in the future.

CHAPTER 7

Non-Structural Repairs

The home service

I could have headed this chapter 'maintenance', but the sad and honest truth is that we pretty much don't do maintenance anymore. I think it went out of fashion with taking shoes to the cobblers. Now, we wait for things to break, and then fix them. Sometimes we wait for things to break, wait a bit longer still, and then – and only then as an absolute last resort – do we begin to think about fixing them. This is partly because in this age we are all so busy that unless something is seriously wrong we won't spend much of our valuable time on it, and partly because when the property market is as buoyant as it often is, it seems that any old wreck of a building is a treasure. I blame estate agents, home-improvement TV shows and MDF – in that order: collectively they have led us to believe that so long as the inner décor of our homes looks nice, the structure behind it can be left to the verge of collapse, making us happy to throw money in bucketloads at our kitchens and bathrooms, but not spend a penny on fixing a leaking gutter.

If you plan on spending your life hopping from one place to another, maybe you never will have to carry out maintenance. But homes are like cars: if you want to keep them for a while and they aren't regularly serviced, sooner or later they are going to let you down.

If the place offers us sanitation with shelter and warmth, cold and hot water, and is nicely decorated we can live with it (or, to be more accurate, in it). But when defects do occur, if they don't immediately affect our standard of living, they are often put to the back of the list of things demanding our attention. What we need to recognise is that it is relatively easy and cheap to do minor repairs regularly, but the consequences of not doing them can be a lot more expensive. In the same way that not changing the cam belt on your car can lead it to snap and wreck your entire engine, a leaking rainwater pipe can saturate the ground, eventually weakening the soil and causing subsidence, or a loose wire may cause an earth leakage and start a fire. Maintaining your home in good order will maintain its value, even when the market is bad, and avoid much worse problems later on.

So what I'm suggesting is, and you might want to steady yourself against some cushions here, is to keep a simple maintenance plan. A plan of nothing fancy, nothing expensive, but basic and essential maintenance that could save you money in the long term. A logbook for your home can contain this plan and the dates of when each task was last attended to, just as the service book for your car does. At the risk of sounding like a pyramid salesman, you can break the plan down into three parts: annual maintenance, five-year maintenance and ten-year maintenance.

If you've recently moved into your home, now is the time for the first of your five- and ten-year checks, particularly if you didn't have a structural survey before buying.

141

Annual maintenance

These are the minor tasks that just need attending to once a year to keep your home shipshape and up to scratch. They should include the following basic elements, but you may have specific parts of your home that need to be added to the list.

Drainage system

Check inside manholes to see that they remain clean and in good condition. Sometimes internal rendered walls of manholes can become cracked. In time pieces of render will fall and block the drains, so it is best to remove it before this happens. We don't render manholes internally these days because of this, but if your chamber walls are built from a soft brick or are only a half-brick thick, you will have to renew the render to keep them watertight.

Rainwater system

Clean out rainwater gutters, hoppers and pipes. Moss and dirt can accumulate quickly in gutters, after all they are there to take the wash off the roof, and it's amazing how much can build up in them in just one year. Regular clean-outs can be done with a ladder and hosepipe, but if left for too many years, a trowel will be needed to dig them out.

At the same time check to see that the joints in the system aren't leaking or whether any brackets have become loose. Gutters will sag if brackets fail or are too far apart, especially plastic gutters, which do have the advantage of being easy to keep clean and will flow freely with the slightest of falls, but as every burglar will tell you, they are extremely weak and come away at the slightest provocation. A cold winter with snow and ice can do a lot of damage to plastic guttering, and if this is a regular occurrence where you live, you might want to add some extra brackets to your gutters to reduce their span between supports. Spring is a good time to check them. Conservatories have systemised guttering along with the rest of their kit-build parts, so that you can easily clip on extra brackets for the guttering and slide them along for centring at whatever spacings you might want.

If your home has cast-iron gutters, look for signs of rusting with old age. It's inevitable that at some point they may need to be replaced, and if this becomes necessary, you might want to consider the virtues of doing so in plastic or aluminium.

Aluminium gutters are rustproof and lightweight, and can sometimes make an acceptable replacement, even when used in Conservation Areas. Plastic usually isn't appropriate on listed buildings, but for the rest of us, it has the advantage of coming in a variety of shapes and sizes, and the flow capabilities are extremely variable. If your present gutter, even if it is in good order, really can't cope with a downpour, it might be worth replacing it with a more efficient type. You can also improve the efficiency of your system by repositioning the downpipe in the middle of the gutter, rather than at one end, although this will obviously mean extending the below-ground drainage system to meet it.

GUTTER FLOW RATE TABLE

	68 mm		68 mm	
	Downpipe in centre		Downpipe at end	
Gutter shape	Flow	Roof area	Flow	Roof area
Half round 112 mm	2.6	125	1.3	62
Half round 125 mm	4.6	221	2.4	115
Square	3.8	182	2.0	96
Ogee style	3.0	144	1.5	72

NOTES:
Examples only – manufacturers will give exact figures for their own products
Flow rates quoted in litres per second
Roof areas quoted in square metres
Assumes gutters fixed at a fall of 1/350
Assumes roof pitches up to 50°
Assumes 75 mm/hr rainfall (National Annual Rainfall Intensity figure)

You can calculate the area of your pitched roof by adding the width of the roof (measured on plan) between the ridge and the eaves to half the height of the roof, and then multiplying this figure to the length of the roof. If you have a 90° bend in the gutter, add on 10 per cent to the area.

Airbricks and vents
Check that your airbricks and vents aren't obstructed. In properties with suspended timber ground floors, it is essential to keep a flow of air beneath the floor. Without it the air becomes stagnant, and an environment for wet or dry rot is created. Since air bricks for floors are often at outside ground level on older homes (new ones use periscope-style vents that turn up inside the cavity of the cavity wall), they are prone to becoming clogged with dirt and moss, if not actually buried entirely beneath paths and patios.

Air vents aren't just used for floors, however; they play an essential role in providing combustion air for fires and oil, gas or solid-fuel appliances. Combustion air is the oxygen needed to keep a fire burning; without it, the flame or pilot light expires and the lethal gas carbon monoxide can escape into the room. If you have a vent at low level in your home that is causing a draught,

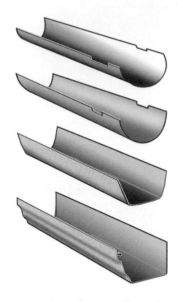

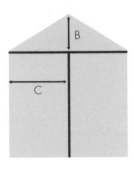

$$C + \frac{B}{2} \times \text{length of roof} = \text{effective roof area}$$

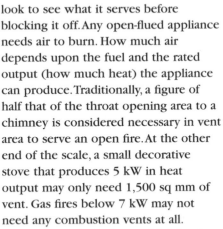

Types of gutter with different flow capacities.

Calculating effective roof area.

look to see what it serves before blocking it off. Any open-flued appliance needs air to burn. How much air depends upon the fuel and the rated output (how much heat) the appliance can produce. Traditionally, a figure of half that of the throat opening area to a chimney is considered necessary in vent area to serve an open fire. At the other end of the scale, a small decorative stove that produces 5 kW in heat output may only need 1,500 sq mm of vent. Gas fires below 7 kW may not need any combustion vents at all.

Vents are always best at high level, above head height, where they are less of a nuisance and less likely to be covered, but louvres can be fitted to them to deflect control their airflow. If you don't have the correct amount of ventilation to a gas appliance, the

supply company can disconnect the appliance and prohibit its use.

Roof tiles

Check the roof covering to see whether any slates or tiles have slipped or broken. A visual inspection can be done from a ladder or from the ground with a pair of binoculars.

Do not invite itinerant roofers to inspect the roof for you and offer their services. If you invite quotes for roof repairs, make sure you invite a few and compare them; ask how many tiles are damaged and need to be replaced.

Roof tiles and slates come to an age when they can become porous and attract lichen and moss. In itself this isn't a problem, but if the whole roof is really beginning to green up, you can clean it with a fungicidal spray or brush-on solution – the same stuff sold for cleaning paths and patios can be used on roof tiles. If you find that once cleaned, the tiles have faded and lost their colour and finish, you can go one step further by having them painted. Roof-tile paints are specialised acrylic polymer-based coatings that can be brushed onto a clean and dry roof. These products can transfer an old weathered roof into a shiny, bright-new-pin roof with a permanent wet look, so if this isn't what you want, you should steer clear of them.

Repairing flashings and valley gutters

Lead flashings around chimneys and lead coverings to dormer and other flat roofs are also prone to suffer in the long term. Often flashings may just need to be dressed back down after the wind has lifted them, but when cracked and split they should be replaced. Cement mortar has at times been used as a cheap alternative to lead, but it doesn't last nearly as long and will become damaged by frost. Code 4 lead is used around abutments like chimneys as flashings (which overdress the tiles) and soakers (which underdress the tiles).

Valleys are the intersections between two interlinking roof pitches. This makes them the place where rainfall is channelled and where snow can build up, and hence the very place where problems can occur with weathering. They can be formed and weathered in a few different ways: with V-shaped valley tiles that continue tiling without breaking the course or cutting the tiles, with cut tiling and a lead lining, or now in fibreglass to form a gutter.

Lead is graded by its code numbers, which represent the weight of it in pounds per square foot – needless to say, this doesn't convert to metric very well, so it has been left that way. There is also a colour coding with the wrapping, which helps to identify it.

LEAD CODE	COLOUR CODE	THICKNESS
3	Green	1.32 mm
4	Blue	1.80 mm
5	Red	2.24 mm
6	Black	2.65 mm
7	White	3.15 mm
8	Orange	3.55 mm

Either way valleys need supporting – it isn't sufficient to just let the tiling battens run over the last rafter and carry the weight. Timber boards were traditionally used to form a shuttering base across the rafters for the lead to be dressed to; if the valley has leaked for some years, this could be affected by wet rot and need replacing. More often than not it will be just a case of re-lining the valley with lead. Lead expands beneath the heat of the sun, and to allow for this expansion the new material should be seated on underlay material that it won't stick to, and formed in bays of a given length. These bays are then overlapped at steps, dependent on the code size and girth (width) of the lead, as shown in the table above.

LEAD CODE	MIN STEP (DRIP) HEIGHT	MAX LENGTH OF BAY	MAX OVERALL GIRTH
4	50 mm	1500 mm	750 mm
5	50 mm	2000 mm	800 mm
6	50 mm	2250 mm	850 mm
7	60 mm	2500 mm	900 mm
8	60 mm	3000 mm	1000 mm

● Code 4 lead is the minimum grade for use in gutters, but because the lengths are limited to only 1.5 m, code 5 is more commonly used

● The minimum fall along lead-lined gutters should be 1:80. Falls of steeper than 1:60 should receive improved nail fixings to prevent slippage

● Tapered gutters should not be less than 150 mm wide at their narrowest or lowest point

Glassfibre (GRP) valley troughs are becoming a popular alternative to traditional lead linings; although the material is thin, it may not creep so much as lead on hot, sunny days, and it comes preformed in standard lengths that can be overlapped and sealed with silicone mastic, However, lead gutters have one distinctive benefit over GRP – they allow access for cleaning. You can walk up them if need be without fear of damaging them or yourself; GRP is likely to split if you tried, but the narrower width polished surface is going to make

it a hazardous ascent anyway. All things considered, it is best to reserve the plastic for steeper and more inaccessible gutters, such as those at the intersection of opposing steep roofs. It goes without saying that plastic gutters don't suit listed buildings or Conservation Areas any more than plastic windows do. In fact, they look out of sorts on pretty well anything but post-1960 homes.

Have gas appliances checked

Gas appliances should be checked annually by a CORGI-registered plumber or gas fitter. This inspection can be a visual check plus testing the emissions from the flue to see if the appliance is burning cleanly and expelling its waste gases effectively. Gas boilers or fires that aren't can leak carbon monoxide into the room. This gas is invisible, tasteless and odourless, and the first way that people usually become aware of its presence is by feeling drowsy and lethargic. Carbon monoxide poisoning is a slow, gradual process, but a fatal one nevertheless. Appliances that are inspected and revealed to be dangerous in their condition are decommissioned and labelled as unfit for use.

Some gas suppliers offer service contracts that include an annual inspection with an insurance-based warranty for the heating and hot water system. These may only be available on relatively new installations, and can be riddled with exclusions for such things as hard water area defects. If you live in the Southeast, for example, almost any failure of your plumbing system, pumps, valves, etc., can be attributed to hard water, and so you may find these contracts unworthy. Check the details before signing up.

Five-year maintenance
Repointing

A walk around the outside of your home to view the brickwork is all that is needed to see if the mortar joints between the bricks are in good order; deeply recessed mortar joints can reduce the strength of walls by up to half. Use a penknife to scrape at the joints, even if they aren't recessed, to see that they have not become powdery and damageable with light abrasion.

You should not forget to check below DPC (damp-proof course), where walls are particularly vulnerable to damp. With time and exposure, mortar wears to the point where it becomes either so recessed into the brickwork that it no longer weathers the wall, or becomes loose with rain and frost action, making it crack and fall out. Either way it can be easily repointed. Damaged joints first have to be raked out and cleaned thoroughly before the fresh mortar is used to refill them.

Repointing after raking out joints.

The trick with repointing is to try and blend the new mortar in with the existing mortar. If you are only working on parts of the wall, the mix ratio of cement, sand and lime can be varied on sample areas to achieve a match. The ratio of the mix will affect the hardness and colour of the joints. Bricklaying sand can come in a variety of colours, from white to yellow to orange, and in some areas red – all of them are natural, but the colour depends on where they were quarried. The colour of the sand used is the same, so you may want to experiment with a few different mixes first to see how close you can get to matching before you really get stuck into it.

Have electrical circuits tested

Electrical circuits can be tested for earth leaks and polarity by qualified electricians armed with the right equipment. Your electrician will provide you with an inspection and test certificate to confirm that your wiring is satisfactory, and a report should indicate which circuits and sub-circuits have been examined and tested. It is fairly labour-intensive work in large properties where a number of circuits exist, but according to the ECA (Electrical Contractors Association) you can expect to pay for 30 minutes of labour for each sub-circuit and between 20 and 30 minutes per final circuit. If you're planning on renting a property out, you may need to have an annual inspection and relevant test certificate provided to comply with the law.

The condition of the fuse holders and the distribution board should also be noted. Prior to the mid-1980s when miniature circuit breakers (MCBs) replaced them, fuses were used in pull-out fuse holders on our boards. If they have been frequently pulled for maintenance on the circuits over the years, they may have become damaged; they do seem to have been made from a brittle plastic. You should still be able to replace these holders with new ones, but they are becoming scarce, so in the long run it could prove wise to have the board changed for a MCB, easily popped out by push-button action and reset. If you do stick with replacing fuses and fuse-holders, you should note the colour coding for each fuse rating, e.g. white for 5-amp, blue for 15-amp, red for 30-amp; although the holders are made in different sizes to prevent incorrect ratings being used, you should keep them labelled with a note of which circuits they serve.

The trouble with electrics is that they can work without being safe. Earth leakages can result in fires, often in undetected areas like roof spaces, but an inspection of the circuits might also reveal loose connections to fittings, outlets and junction boxes. It might also draw attention to nailed-through wiring (I am given to understand that there has been at least one death caused by somebody standing on a live nail and touching a radiator) and insufficient cable size; here, cables are overloaded beyond their capacity, causing them to overheat. Incorrectly rated fuses or MCBs and reversed polarity are other favourite nasties.

Inspection and testing of electrical work is covered within the IEE Wiring Regulations (No. 3 of a set of seven guidance notes).

Damp inspection

You can expect to find damp below DPC level on your external walls, but DPC level should not be higher than finished floor level inside your home; so if you have signs of damp on inside walls, you have a problem.

The DPC is usually visible somewhere along the external brickwork. It should be above ground level by at least two courses of bricks – any less places it at risk of being bridged by rain splashing or groundwater. If you can't find it easily, trace the course joint around from directly beneath the doorsill, as the DPC is commonly bedded at this level during construction, with the doorsill placed on it. You may have to scrape away a bit of mortar to reveal the edge. In older properties slate was used as the DPC, then bitumen and now plastic.

Rising damp results from an absent or bridged DPC, and is easily treated in masonry by a chemical-injection process. But damp has other causes, ranging from high exposure to wind-driven rain, leaking downpipes and gutters and, inside your home, condensation.

If you have damp walls internally, black mould can appear on the surface, wallpaper can relentlessly fail to stick, paint can bubble and blister on the plaster, and the wall can seem cold and damp to the touch. A suitably qualified independent surveyor can, armed with a moisture meter, inspect and advise whether the wall is suffering from just surface dampness (likely to be caused by condensation) or is a damp structure. Cavity-fill insulation can cause damp by bridging the cavity if it hasn't been installed cleanly and completely, and this problem can only be rectified by its removal from the cavity at the site of the damp. The cavity should be left ventilated to dry out before being cleaned and re-filled with insulation.

Do not rely on inspection by remedial DPC companies to determine the cause of dampness. Their surveys may be 'free', but form part of the product they are anxious to sell to you. Ideally for them, rising damp treated with an injected chemical DPC and hacked off and re-plastered walls inside will form the cure. It's their product, they want to sell it to you. Other problems that may be causing damp are likely to be out of their sphere of business curewise, and hence are of no interest to them. It might just be a case of reducing the ground level outside one wall or fixing a leaking gutter.

Prune trees

The roots of trees growing too close to your home can be contained by pruning the branches. Pollarding has the same effect – cut back the growth of the tree and you cut back the growth of its roots and the effect they could have on your foundations. In clay soils it is very important to guard against the risk of subsidence from soil desiccation, but in any soil, trees too close to your home and its drains can cause damage. Pollarding is the act of cutting back to the main trunk or the main trunk and bows; in the case of large trees, once every five years should keep them in check. However, faster-growing small trees and even shrubs need to be pruned every year.

Ten-year maintenance
Ground level

Check the outside ground level and the height of the DPC. Ground levels have a habit of changing over time, and so this check is aimed at making sure the ground levels around your home haven't been raised to less than 150 mm below the DPC. Gardening on poor soils encourages people to import topsoil and compost to overdress the ground. Pathways and patios may have been surface-laid by previous owners not keen on starting the job by reducing the ground level, and it is painfully common to see them up at DPC level, allowing rain to wash over the course.

You needn't dig up the whole patio if this is the case; cutting it back away from the walls is usually enough. Half a slab back or even 150 mm away, a circular stone-cutting saw can slice out a drainage channel that can be dug down to the required depth below the DPC. A little soft filling with 10 mm stone should keep it free-draining, but otherwise a drainage channel should be exactly that, a channel. You can buy gratings in sectional gutter-style channels, but they need to run to a suitable drain.

Test drains for leaks

Drains can be tested for leaks - you don't have to wait for them to reveal themselves through foundation subsidence. All you need is to hire some basic drain-testing equipment or a plumber with some, and persuade your family not to use any of the facilities for half an hour.

Drain plugs are rubber seals that can be expanded by turning a screw to grip the open end of a drainpipe: two are needed, one at each end in a manhole or the top of a soil vent pipe, together with a tube gauge called a manometer to check the pressure in the pipe. A leak in air pressure will reveal a leak in the pipe. Water tests can also be carried out on the drains below ground by filling the drainage from a manhole with water and seeing if the level drops over a period of time. You really need to leave a water test on for at least 15 minutes and mark the water line on the side of the manhole with chalk to see if it has dropped from its original level.

Repainting outside woodwork

This task has driven half the country into plastic window ownership. It must rank number one on the list of unpopular maintenance tasks, and so anything you can do to make it less frequent should interest you. If you prefer wood - and plenty of people do - it is worth taking time to prepare it thoroughly by sanding down and preparing it for painting. Timber that has been primed and undercoated with two coats, each lightly sanded and then glossed in two coats, won't need to be repainted for a decade. Timber that is half-heartedly sanded and glossed over will need redoing in two or three years.

Microporous paints are breathable and should also extend the longevity of the finish, but I can't stress enough the fact that the longer you spend on preparing for the gloss finish, the longer it will be before you do the job again.

Having advised you to take off the old before starting again, you need to judge how old the old is. If your home was built prior to 1960 and the woodwork has been over-painted since then, the original coat may still be lurking underneath. Before 1960, when the world was less troubled by issues of health and safety, white lead was the principal pigment in household paint. If you try to remove the paint by power sanding or burning, the lead will be released to cause contamination and potential harm; young children and expectant mums are the most vulnerable to the effects of lead. If you're not certain whether your paint is lead-based, it can be easily tested with a swab kit available from your local paint or builders' merchant.

The use of chemical strippers is the safest way to strip paint, although it is also possible to soften it gently with an electric heat gun so that it can be

Windows, doors and skirting boards
Wood should be treated with vacuum-applied preservative, then a solvent-based wood primer and two undercoats and finished with two gloss coats.
Fascias, barge boards and soffits
Wood should be treated with a vacuum-applied preservative, breathable primer, two undercoats and two gloss coats of microporous paint or stain system.

carefully scraped away. All debris should be carefully removed before you begin repainting, and a plastic sheet spread out below the work area will help to catch it. This is not a job for a windy day. The HSE and the Paintmakers Association will be pleased to give you further advice (see their contact details on the back pages).

With any painted timber, and definitely with fascia and soffit boards, I would resist the temptation to burn it with a blowtorch. It is surprisingly easy to set fire to the wood, and on more than one occasion I can think of, this has resulted in burning the roof down.

Roof repairs
Repairing flat roofs
Flat roofs need to be looked after. The traditional method of using three layers of bitumen-based roofing felt bonded together works well in the short term,

but only if the water runs off effectively in winter and the surface reflects the sun in summer – which is historically where it all has gone wrong, with rainwater pools in flat spots forming on the roof and the mineral chippings becoming loose in time and disappearing for good.

The result from either or both of these events is that the felt cracks and splits and ultimately leaks. Re-covering the entire roof is usually what is needed. Luckily, some advances have been made in materials for flat roofing, and more advanced products are now on the market.

If your felt roof looks a little old and tired on the surface, with the chippings worn a bit thin, you might think about having it refurbished. Even a fresh topping of mineral chippings will help, but you now have the choice of chippings or solar reflective paint. This paint is usually silver and somewhat visible from above, but then its job is to send back most of the sunlight hitting it. Even so, I can't imagine the consequences if every roof in the country was covered with it.

Some products are based on a mixture of bitumen, rubber and fibre reinforcement with a solar reflective quality designed into them, and are used for repairing minor leaks and damaged roofs as well as renewing that sun protection. Bear in mind that these are close to instant repairs at the low end of the market, which usually means temporary repairs, so you need to think about how long you want them to work for before deciding on a solution.

Re-covering flat roofs

The roof you are seeking to repair is more than likely a multi-ply roof, like the built-up felt systems of bitumen felt. Some single-ply systems can be used to re-cover these, rather than have to rip them off and start from the decking material again. The existing material will need to be dry and relatively clean and is going to need some preparation in this respect, but once done a high-polymer membrane can be unrolled over it and the joints welded together.

PVC is used in an elasticised form that, when laid and jointed, creates a homogenous cover. You have to buy the purpose-made edge trims and bits for wall abutments, but otherwise the system is wonderfully simple since it can be bonded to existing bitumen or asphalt roofs. But here's the thing: in order for the manufacturers to guarantee their product, they will only allow it to be installed by registered roofers and, like the poured fibreglass equivalents which come with anything up to 30-year guarantees, you have to appoint a specialist and approved contractor. Most fibreglass products have a polished battleship grey finish to them that looks wet even when it's dry – they look neat and watertight, and they are neat and watertight, but unfortunately they also mimic the appearance of the helicopter landing pad on HMS Ark Royal.

I am not a fan of flat roofs, and personally I don't think that there is anything that you can use to make them look attractive, except possibly by installing a roof garden.

Pitched roof repairs

Loose and cracked tiles on pitched roofs are easy to replace. With concrete interlocking tiles, only one course in five or more may be actually nailed down, and it is the work of a few minutes to lift them and replace with new matching tiles. The manufacturers have continued to make tiles they introduced in the 1970s and after, so there shouldn't be any reason why you can't find replacements. The only thing is the colour – old tiles fade, and new ones will look a little obvious until they weather in. If you repeatedly seem to lose ridge, verge or hip tiles during strong winds, you might decide to replace them with a dry-clipped system instead of simply bedding them in mortar. Dry systems are mechanically fixed down, anchored to the ridge boards, verges and hip rafters.

To re-cover a roof entirely only becomes necessary when the covering has become badly worn or, more commonly, when the fixings have corroded; nail sickness is the term for the latter. Asbestos slates are often replaced with cement fibre slates, and when re-covering an entire roof, it is customary to replace the felt with a modern untearable underlay. Breathable perforated felts are used to help disperse vapour in the loft space and avoid condensation. New slates or tiles will mean new battens at the correct gauge in any case; check that the joints are staggered with them on trussed rafter roofs, and are not vertical for more than five courses.

In the case of asbestos cement slates, the asbestos content is between 10 and

15 per cent, but more importantly it is bound and compacted in and is therefore only harmful when broken. Dropping the tiles off the roof is a common problem, as in doing so fibres can be released and become airborne.

Why are asbestos fibres such a threat? Because inhaling them can lead to diseases of the lungs and chest, like cancer. The more fibres that are breathed in, the higher the risk of disease; some 3000 deaths occur annually in Britain as a result of asbestos-related diseases.

Your roofers will need to work in accordance with the Health and Safety Executive's guidelines and have liability insurance cover for this type of work and training certification – evidence of these should be requested. The old slates should be removed after being carefully bagged into double-layer polythene sacks, labelled and taken to a licensed waste disposal site that accepts them. Household waste sites do not normally have a facility for dealing with asbestos, but your local authority or nearest HSE office will know where the closest site to you is.

Underspray foam system

I am tempted not to mention this, I really am, but that wonder product of the Millennium, polyurethane foam, has also found its way, not surprisingly, into the roof repair market. Yes, men in white overalls can be sent into your attic to spray the ever-expanding gunk between your rafters with spray guns. A bit like the polystyrene ceiling tiles we lovingly coated our kitchen ceilings with once, yellow polyurethane foam can line the inside of our pitched roofs, insulating it and sticking every part of your roof together.

I assume that the foam's place in the market is with old roofs that lack underlay felt or boarding beneath the tiles, and with cut rafters. Once set, the insulant would bond the roof together, affording it some wind resistance and hence strengthening it at least in one direction, but it would also insulate it to create a warm roof space, sealed against draughts and weather. If an underlay does exist, it is going to have to be removed to allow the foam to be sprayed against the underside of the roof covering. To avoid the unfortunate event of foam oozing out and over your roof, giving it the 'Amityville House' look, loose or missing tiles will need to be fixed beforehand.

Underspray foam treatment of close-boarded roof.

Because this stuff sticks like really sticky stuff to a blanket, it bonds the tiles together, relieving nail sickness, or nail fatigue if you prefer, and more or less guaranteeing no more slipped tiles. Of course, anyone wanting to strip the roof tiles in the future to replace them with something different is going to be cursing you like a demon as they try to prise the tiles off. Products like these must be the exact opposite of sustainable repair.

The manufacturers must have had some vision of what we, the public, would do with this foam's availability in a large quantity from a DIY store, so it only comes as a system application via an approved contractor.

Wall repairs
Window repairs and re-glazing
Expanding foam and silicone mastic are excellent materials for filling and sealing gaps around the frames of windows and doors. Although these products come from a variety of manufacturers at a variety of prices and all look the same, they aren't – professionals have learnt the hard way that you have to buy quality if you want the products to be weatherproof and durable.

Replacing panes of cracked glass shouldn't be a problem if the frames are sound. Traditional putty may have become brittle and cracked, so replace it with acrylic putty, which should stay flexible for much longer. Given a different style of window, hardwood glazing beads pinned and bedded in acrylic putty are ideal.

Repairs to glazing are not covered under the Building Regulations in the same way that replacing windows and doors are. The type of glass you use in repairs can be identical to what was there previously, although it may be prudent to replace it with something stronger if it's in a vulnerable position. Low-level glass (below 800 mm above the floor level) and glass in doors and sidelights is considered to be at risk from accidental impact. In these critical areas toughened or laminated glass should be used, although annealed glass, hardened in the manufacturing process, can be just as good in small panes like French windows.

When it comes to glazing repairs, the frame will determine the thickness and, to some extent, the type of glass you use, plus of course the desire to match it with the existing panes. It is surprising how different glass can look, given the types now available, from polished to cast plate, toughened to laminated and single- to double-glazed with low-emissivity coating. The light reflecting off the glass will soon reveal it to be different from the rest, so if you can't match it you may wish to replace all the panes in a window or door.

Just to remind you, laminated glass is the type that comprises layers bonded together, which means that it cracks but won't shatter, making it ideal for security. Because of this it is inherently thicker than toughened glass, which shatters safely into tiny squares when broken, rather than sharp, jagged splinters like plate glass. Laminated glass is used in car windscreens, while toughened glass is used for the side windows.

If you are employing a glazier, it

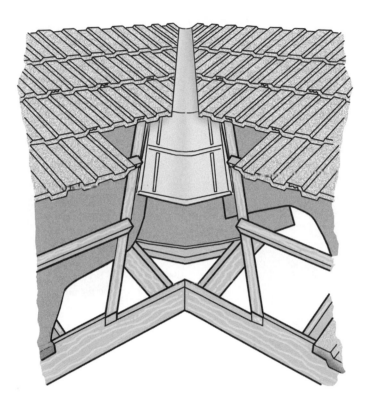

Lead lining replacement to valley gutter.

helps to find one who is registered with the Glass and Glazing Federation and sporting the GGF label. They have a code of both ethical and technical standards for their members, as well as providing a back-up advisory service, although you should bear in mind that ultimately they are a trade association like any other.

Drainage repairs
Blockages
Quite understandably, we choose to avoid thinking about drains until they become blocked and our waste water refuses to part with our company, at which time they occupy our immediate attention. Kitchen sinks are prone to becoming blocked, given the oils, fats and bits of food that get washed down them. If you're lucky, a sink plunger (a stick with a big rubber sucker on the end) will be all that it takes to unlock it and let the water away. Make sure you run some hot water into the sink before plunging the plughole, as this will help

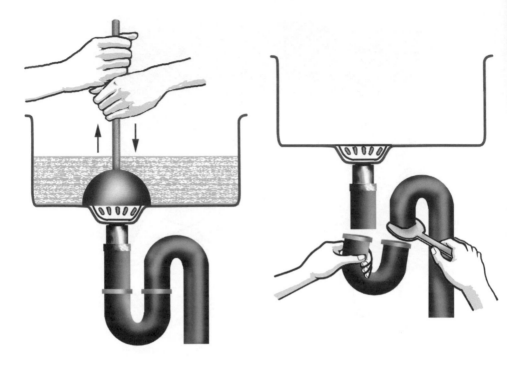

Plunger method of unblocking a sink.   Removing the waste trap.

provide the suction seal. Failing this, a bowl beneath the sink waste and a careful unscrewing of the waste trap will be needed. The trap contains 75 mm depth of water, so be aware of this when you take it off.

Invariably it is the bends to the trap that become blocked, but if the waste pipework itself is where the problem lies, a hosepipe or, better still, a drain auger that you can turn to work out the blockage, is the answer. This is a messy job, and it's always tempting to pour a heavy dose of chemical drain cleaner down it instead, but these products are based on caustic soda and bauxite, among other nasties, and for sinks at

least, rubber gloves and manual cleaning are far better.

Plungers can work equally well on WC pans that have become blocked in the trap, but flexible rods or a short length of hosepipe that can be fed through it and pulled in and out to work the blockage free are more often effective. Shower traps tend to block periodically with detergents and hairs, and the plumbing industry has produced removable traps that can be released and lifted out for cleaning.

Below-ground drains are usually best left to drain-cleaning specialists who tend to use high-pressure cleaning, rather than drain rods. The rods, which are still available for hire, come in short sections and are screwed together to form yards of semi-rigid pole. A selection of head fittings for the business end collectively create the corkscrew (working your way through blockage), the plunger (coming through regardless of blockage, and shoving the problem further down the run) or the discerning hook end, which drags the problem back to you (for your own piece of mind and also for any onlookers' entertainment).

Some people, not many but a rare and select few, seem to find so much gratification in blocked drains that they can't contain their interest. You'll recognise them immediately by the way they continue to stare fixedly into blocked-up manholes long after everybody else has risked a glance. They are rarely so happy as when they up to their knees in sewage, and these are the people you should look for in the drain-cleaning business, even if they do insist on letting you know exactly what the cause of the blockage was.

Root damage to drainage pipes.

While most people are anxious to clear a blocked sewer, a leaking sewer can be another matter.

Repairing drainage

Most defects concerning homes can be left for a time while we think about the repairs and prepare ourselves for the cost of them, but not drains. Drains that either leak or are blocked and threaten to spill over, are a health risk, and time is not on your side. Because of this, your local authority has considerable powers under the Building Act 1984 to ensure that drains with problems are not left unattended for long.

You can easily divide drains into two categories: those that you are responsible for, and those that you are not. The hard part comes from deciding which are which. Many homes share drainage systems that collect the water from each property as they run, before delivering it out to the public sewer. Public sewers are owned by the regional water authorities, and they are responsible for upkeep and maintenance, wherever the drains may run. I say this because while the majority of public sewers are under our roads, some run beneath our gardens and occasionally our homes.

All public sewers are marked as such on maps, digital for the most part now, and these are held by the water authority and the local council for public inspection. Digital maps can normally be viewed with some assistance at your local authority offices, and sometimes copies can be purchased. The beauty of them is you can zoom in on the part of the sewer you have an interest in, and identify its size and depth along with its position.

If the sewer isn't shown as a public one according to these records, you have only one last chance of it being the water authority's responsibility. Main drain runs that are shared by two or more homes built before 1934 are described as Section 24 sewers under the Public Health Act, and these too fall under the water authority's responsibility. It's worth knowing this if they ever become blocked or leak and have to be repaired, because you and your neighbours shouldn't have to pay. However (why is there always a 'however'?), the drains that connect your home to this shared drain, in other words those that solely serve your home and nobody else's, are your responsibility and yours alone. All other drains shown on the public sewer record are private.

Shared drains

Shared drainage systems are still commonly installed today. Developers building new housing estates do not go to the trouble of connecting each home individually to the public sewer. Instead, they feed a common drain around the gardens of several homes, collecting each as they go, before leading it out to the adoptable sewer. This common drain becomes the joint responsibility of all those homes that connect to it, and this is represented in the deeds for those properties concerned.

In a perfect world, when a problem occurs with this drain, all the affected home-owners link hands and skip towards solving the problem harmoniously, and share out the costs of doing so fairly and proportionally. Where it doesn't happen quite that way – when one or some of the neighbours don't get on quite so well, or where one person is left to sort out the problem for everybody simply because the blockage has occurred on their land, or because (in my case) they have drain cleaning rods in their shed – goodwill is often relied upon. If goodwill is in short supply and nothing is being done by anyone to solve the problem, any of the home-owners along the blocked or broken run can lodge a complaint with the Environmental Health section of the local council.

Environmental Health Officers have powers under the Building Act 1984 to serve notices on each of the responsible property owners, requiring them to resolve the problem collectively and within 48 hours. Invariably they will trace the drain run and the homes on it upstream of the blockage, visiting each owner to advise them. The 48 hours bit is worth mentioning, because the controlling legislation specifies it and makes a point of saying it shouldn't be any less or any more. Blocked drainage demands an element of urgency. If the notices do not unite the owners into sharing the problem and its solution, and the sewer remains blocked after 48 hours, the local authority can step in – probably literally by then – and unblock it themselves. They then should serve follow-up notices to the owners, advising them of their intention to recover the costs from them, apportioned equally to each. Since they are likely to add their administrative expenses to their drain-cleaning bill, it can prove to be the least economical way of resolving the problem. In short, it pays to get on with your neighbours when you share their drains.

When drain blockages re-occur frequently, you really need to discover why, and the only effective way to do this is to commission a camera survey of the system. Video camcorders on miniaturised go-carts are released into the drain at the manholes and sent trundling off under remote control. Equipped with lights and attached by cable, they are able to relay live pictures back to a TV monitor, enabling the viewer to see where defects in the pipes occur. Although the robot's progress is necessarily slow and without commercial breaks, the pictures make for surprisingly interesting viewing. The image is recorded to videotape, and because it is electronically stencilled with the distance along the drain it has travelled, the damaged parts of the pipe can be exactly plotted for repair.

Below-ground repairs

Repairs of below-ground drains can be disruptive. If large sections of pipe are broken or out of level, it will usually be a case of digging them up and re-laying them. If the damage is more isolated, a holed pipe for example, techniques do exist to re-line pipes internally. 'For goodness sake, how?' you ask. I'm pleased you did, because it's actually pretty cool: they feed this other little robot thingy along the pipe to the spot where the hole is, to deliver a drain repair sleeve thingy (stop me if I'm getting too technical, won't you), which is then expanded out to seal the pipe from the inside. The material is thin enough not to cause any blockages itself and yet strong enough to render the drain watertight. All you need is a period of time when the drain can't be used to effect the repairs. Once again in a shared system, local authorities have powers to carry these measures out themselves (after serving notice) and to recover the costs.

Replacing defective drains

Not everybody is thrilled by the prospect of digging up the garden to replace broken drains; it's relatively slow, messy work that draws in the opportunity of damaging patios, plants

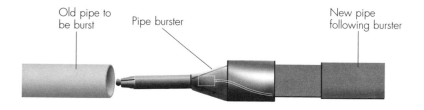

Pipe bursting.

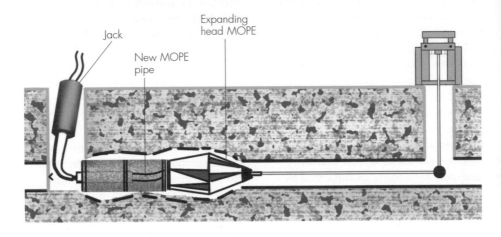

Jack

New MOPE pipe

Expanding head MOPE

Pipe bursting.

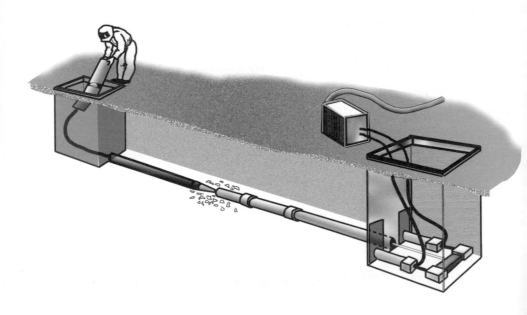

Access via manholes – pipe bursting requires no digging.

and fencing. If you fall into this category, you might want to explore the possibility of the pipe-bursting method. Pipe bursting is not nearly as exciting as it sounds, but it is a specialist procedure and not one your local groundworker will be able to do for you – and like all specialist procedures carried out by specialist companies, it comes complete with a specialist price tag. It is, however, mind-numbingly quick and clean, and doesn't involve anything being dug up, and so the deeper the drain is and the longer the run is, the more attractive this method becomes. The work is usually carried out in a single day, if not half a day.

The burster is a miniature tunnelling machine sent into the drain run from the manhole. It travels along, bursting out the old pipe as it goes and simultaneously laying in the replacement one. It exerts enough pipe-bursting pressure with its head to expand out the diameter of the old drain by up to 600 mm if the ground conditions allow it. The replacement plastic MDPE drain pipe is laid out behind it in 600 mm long jointed sections as it goes, but the process is so fast that up to 100 m can be done in a single day.

Localised repairs

If all your drain needs is repairing in one spot where a hole or broken joint has occurred, repairs are easy enough in shallow-access systems. Most modern homes will have plastic or clay drains laid within 1 m of the surface, generically making them shallow-access systems. Slip collars can be used to replace the damaged pipe with a new piece, after an access hole has been dug and the damaged section cut out. The access hole needs to be big enough for a man to get at the pipe with a pipe cutter or saw, and below about 600 mm

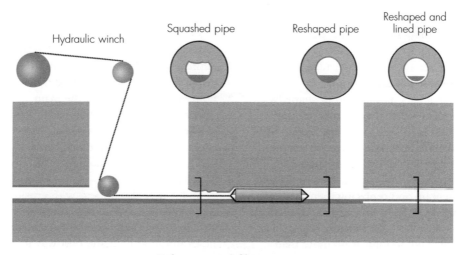

Reforming pitch-fibre pipes.

deep this means working inside an even larger hole.

For deep drainage repairs or where you just don't want a hole dug, patch repairs similar to the pipe replacement system can be done by specialists. Working from the manhole only, the section patch liner is mixed with resin and an inflation tube inserted inside it, which then gets pulled into the pipe to the position of the repair and inflated to a given pressure; the resin sets it in place, and once set, the inflation tube is deflated and removed.

Repairing pitch-fibre drains

Like many of the building products invented in the 1960s, pitch-fibre drains have become something of a liability now. It's difficult to see now why a drainage engineer would think that making drainage pipes out of bitumen was a pretty nifty idea. For centuries before, we'd been using clay, and time had proved it to be strong and durable, but that wasn't good enough for the 1960s building industry, who wanted something new and cheaper. They found it in pitch fibre.

After a few short decades, alas, most of these pipes have either been eaten by rats or squashed out of shape by nothing other than normal ground loads. It seems that a pipe made out of bitumen surprisingly has no strength and won't stay round for very long. Personally I favour the idea of digging them up and replacing them with clay or UPVC, but they can be strengthened by re-lining techniques or just being reshaped. So long as no more than about a third of the pipe has suffered

collapse, it can be re-rounded using a re-rounding device, which is dragged along the run by a hydraulically operated winch. Rocket science doesn't come near it.

Redundant drains and cesspools

Drains are the highway system of rats, but to get in and out of them as often as they like they rely on us to leave openings in the system. With this in mind you might want to replace a broken manhole cover or gully grating that has either enough weight to remain in place under rat attack, or with the type that is screwed down. Lightweight plastic gully gratings should be avoided like the plague, excuse the pun.

It isn't necessary to break out any redundant pipework so long as you seal it off properly at the ends, by which I do not mean tying a plastic bag over it. The only permanent way is to mix up a dry or lean mix of concrete and pack it into the pipe end or redundant manhole to form a permanent plug.

Every so often attention is drawn to a redundant cesspool in the garden by a depression suddenly arriving in the ground. Old tanks, abandoned when the home was connected to the main sewer, were typically filled with rubble and soil, and settlement of this material is gradual but inevitable and can suddenly result in a dramatic difference in ground levels.

Holes may also appear with erosion of soil washed in, and since both rats and children are mysteriously drawn to holes in the ground, the best way to avoid holes is to fill them in and cap them over with a lid of reinforced concrete. A slab can be cast below and the topsoil dressed back over it later.

The cesspool walls are more than likely some metres below normal ground level in any case, and the slab will need casting on top of them. In filling the old tank first, a stone material that will not degrade or consolidate in the future should be used to form a level surface on which to cast the slab. A permanent shutter of 19 mm WPB plywood could be laid across to support the concrete and reinforcement when you are pouring.

Use fabric reinforcement in sheets that if necessary can be overlapped to provide continuous strengthening, and aim to set the sheets some 40 mm or so up from the bottom of the slab. You can use pieces of brick to achieve this if you can't get hold of proprietary ones (known as stools or chairs). The best position for the reinforcing is near the bottom of the concrete slab to resist the tensile stress. Concrete at least 100 mm thick is ideal in combination with a mesh size of A193 or higher grade (a higher number after the 'A' means thicker steel). Most builders' merchants will stock lightweight reinforcement, which is commonly used to strengthen garage floors, but higher grades may have to be ordered in advance or obtained from a steel stockist. Don't be tempted to use chicken wire, which is sometimes employed in floor screeds to resist cracking – it isn't going to achieve much in 100 mm of concrete. If you're disconnecting a cesspool for the first time, it's a good idea to treat it with lime after it has been emptied and washed out, which will help to prevent methane gas from building up.

Cesspool problems

Old cesspools have a habit of existing unnoticed. I mean completely unnoticed. In many older homes, the drainage can be a something of a mystery – it might be known that a cesspool or septic tank of some description serves the property, but nobody is quite sure exactly where it lies or how big it is, because it never gets emptied. The financial implications of leaving it this way forever must be tempting, but the fact is cesspools have to be emptied every few months, and if yours doesn't appear to, then it is probably because it leaks.

The emptying of cesspools is a service usually provided by the local authority, who should have records on when your tank was emptied and how much was pumped out. So if you're new to the property, this information will be of some use to you; apart from telling you whether the thing is leaking or not, it should give you an indication of its storage capacity and how much it costs annually to maintain it.

Undersized tanks that need to be emptied all too frequently (the legal minimum for new tanks is 28 days storage capacity) are effective money pits, and you would do well to replace them with a larger capacity model. Tanks are manufactured out of glassfibre now, and don't leak unless they become physically damaged, but in the past it was traditional to build them from bricks or blocks with rendered walls inside. It is these older-style chambers that have deteriorated over the years and often now leak. Repairing them may only be a matter of replacing a few damaged bricks, but the task of emptying and cleaning out the chamber and leaving it unused to achieve repair usually makes it easier to replace them.

Because defective cesspools are a health hazard and a cause of pollution, local authorities and the Environment Agency have powers to enforce repairs on their owners. The tank need not actually be overflowing or flooding a neighbour's garden with effluent; it can merely be undersized to attract a Repairs Notice from your Environmental Health Office. In practice, most of these problems come to light once they have reached an unpleasant conclusion and the foul water, complete with foul smell, is visible. In these cases a complaint can leave you with a very short period of time to resolve the problem. If you are new to your home, then it's worth taking some time to try and discover the details of your drainage disposal before, one day, the details discover you.

For one unfortunate owner, understanding that his drains were connected to the main sewer was peace of mind enough. Each year he paid his dues to the water authority who owned the sewer until it was ultimately discovered that his drainage hadn't quite made it to the connection; instead it emptied into the ground a few feet short. The sewer spur connection was there, waiting for his pipes to join, but the connection had never been made, leaving him seeking a bit of a refund.

Rainwater problems

It isn't just foul water that sometimes causes us grief; rainwater can be just as troublesome. Soakaways are a cheap solution to rainwater disposal, but often they are poorly built and ineffective in heavy soils. A soakaway that doesn't work is a garden pond that you can't put fish in, and in winter it will easily spill over.

Most domestic soakaways have been built unlined, dug and filled with hardcore; they eventually become silted up and inefficient, and with no way of being cleaned, it is a case of locating them with drain rods down the pipes and digging them out. It makes sense to build soakaways as lined chambers using bricks or precast concrete rings. In this way they can be fitted with manhole covers for access in the future. Open-ended at the base, holes can be augured into the ground at the bottom of the chamber to ease the percolation of the water into the ground. Alternatively, holed linings can be backfilled around the outside with stone, allowing the soakage to occur through the walls of the soakaway. If you have very poor subsoil, such as London clay, it may be better to run an overflow of perforated drainage pipes out from the soakaway as well.

Surface water sewers exist in urban areas sporadically, but on new estates they are more or less always present. It is the water authority's legal duty to provide adequate drainage, and you have a right to connect your rainwater to it. Of course it is known that in many parts of the country such sewers are sadly lacking in capacity and wholly unable to serve the number of homes being connected to them. The byproduct of an overloaded sewer system is flooding, and you my have seen manhole lids popping up after periods of heavy rainfall; for this reason soakaways are often promoted wherever they work effectively – so much so that you may even be eligible for a rebate on your water rates if you can prove that your home is served by soakaways and not the sewer system.

Repairing and maintaining the garden boundary
Fencing

We are indeed fortunate in the British Isles. Having at our disposal a wealth of DIY superstore outlets and builders' merchants, and a number of Bank Holiday weekends to indulge them, is it any wonder that the hotels and beaches are empty? This magical combination allows us to buy cheaply made goods at cheap prices and occupy most of our spare time putting them in place, only to discover that they last only for a few short years before we need to replace them. And replace them we do, with exactly the same cheaply made goods bought at cheap prices – happy in the knowledge that in a few more short years we'll be buying them again.

Take fencing, for example. You can't not have fencing in Britain. Given that we live so close together and that everybody's property borders somebody else's, fencing doesn't just mark our boundaries, it offers us some privacy, until the wind blows harder and the wafer-thin panels we bought bend and disintegrate. I have lost count of the number of fence panels and posts I've bought and replaced in my back garden, but am I at all dissuaded from buying them again? Absolutely not. I could have saved myself some money and a good deal of effort by putting up a stronger fence, but what on earth would I do on Bank Holidays?

Fence posts are the first problem to overcome. A 75 x 75 mm standard softwood fence post has a short life expectancy that is only marginally extended by preservative. In damp ground and set in concrete, four or five years may be all you get before the wet has weakened it enough to snap in the next gale. 150 x 150 mm posts will delay this event considerably, particularly if you can buy them treated and soak the buried section in a silicone-based waterproofer for a day or two before setting it in.

Instead of buying trellis that has been made from matchstick-sized battens stapled together or panels of wafer-thin woven larch, a stout two-rail panel boarded with overlapping feather-edge boards could last for a decade or more if the rails are thick enough at the tenon joints. You have to imagine the wind load on a 2 x 2 m panel being focused into the joints with the posts, and ultimately the posts themselves. Basically, fences are windbreaks, and most aren't strong enough by half. It's this basic design look that brings fences down. In the 1987 hurricane, the strongest fences went down in one piece after the precast concrete posts snapped at ground level. I'm not sure what happened to the weakest, on account of them being entirely absent.

Hedging

Given a bit of patience, we could grow a natural fence that wouldn't rot in the ground, get blown over or ever need staining, it would just need pruning. Hedges might encroach a bit on our valuable land and make plotting the exact boundary a bit tricky, but they are a lot prettier than fences, are much less trouble and are kinder on the environment. Ideal species for gardens are multiple-branching species like box and others:

- **Hawthorn (*Crataegus monogyna*)** The most natural of all hedges and ideal for countryside gardens.

- **Hornbeam (*Carpinus betulus*)** Fast-growing to form an 2.5 m-plus hedgerow that usually keeps hold of its dead leaves in winter.

- **Beech (*Fagus sylvatica*)** Holds its leaves over winter and produces a colourful and thick hedge in time.

- **Yew (*Taxus baccata*)** Slow-growing, but eventually you can achieve a dense but narrow hedge with excellent privacy and protection.

- **Cypress (*Cuppressocyparis*)** The infamous leylandii variety has driven many neighbours to court, and was once on the brink of being outlawed, Its problem is that it is very fast-growing and will achieve 15 m or more if left unpruned. Few of us need the kind of privacy that can screen out a block of flats or the local church. Prune it twice a year, at 2 m high maximum, and more frequently when newly planted, and it should make a neat and dense boundary. Young plants need to be staked to stop the wind whipping them around.

- **Western red cedar (*Thuja plicata*)** Again like the leylandii, you will have problems if you let this one go, because nature intended it to be a tall tree. With an electric hedge-trimmer it can be converted into a thick hedge that will achieve efficient screening, if necessary at a good height. Eventually, if you get fed up with it, you can always cut it down and build a shed from the lumber.

- **Portuguese laurel (*Prunus lusitanica*)** Fast-growing at the rate of up to 375 mm a year to form a very dense windbreak of a hedge with excellent screening.

- **Holly (*Ilex aquifolium*)** A good hedge until it gets old, tall and scraggly, when it starts to thin out at the bottom. Really needs planting with another underplanting species like box to fill in the holes – both should be planted at the same time.

Bear in mind that when you plant any hedge, if you plant along the boundary in a few years you will have created a serious encroachment problem with your neighbour, so set out the planting line with string sufficiently in on your side to allow the hedge to grow. Hedges that have become thin and see-through at the bottom have often done so because the top is wider than the base, overshading it. For a hedge to be impenetrable it needs to be wider at the base than the top, like a buttressed wall. Pruning it correctly in the summer months will help to achieve this.

Hedge-laying

Farmers have been doing this for centuries to keep their hedges strong and thick, keeping in the livestock, but this method can also be used in garden hedges to maintain your privacy and windbreak needs. Branches can be split and folded over laterally with a sharp billhook. Pinned down by stakes that will rot away in time, the layered branches continue to shoot and grow in the spring, rejuvenating the hedge and filling in the holes.

Once established, your hedge will need trimming once or twice a year (depending on the species), but it will never blow down and won't ever need repainting. How good is that?

Glossary

AAV
Air-admittance valve. An anti vacuum valve that allows air in to a plumbing system but none out.

Balanced flue
A room sealed flue that lets in the air supply and out the exhaust gases.

Bargeboard
A timber fascia that runs along the verge of a gable wall.

BEM
Boiler energy manager or weather compensator which controls boiler according to outside and inside air temperatures.

Benching
Cement mortar shoulders inside a manhole either side of the channel.

Bill of quantities
A detailed, item by item account of the building work, measured and priced.

Bonding (plaster)
Lightweight plaster with vermiculite added to for two-coat plastering.

Bonding (electrical)
The earthing of metal pipes and fittings by connecting them to earth wiring to prevent electrical shock.

Breathable construction
Vapour permeable construction that allows moisture as vapour to pass through rather than condense on.

Casement
The hinged and opening part of a window.

Combi boilers
Combination boilers heat water on demand in pressure systems, without the need for storage tanks.

Condensing boilers
High energy efficiency boilers that run at lower temperatures with built in heat exchangers to cool and condense the exhaust gases.

Consumer unit
Also called Distribution Board, panel that holds MCBs or fuses for the home's electrical supply.

Contingency sum
A sum of money retained for unforseen work.

DPM
Damp-proof membrane built in to a concrete floor. Usually polythene but can be liquid bitumen.

Fascia
The board at the eaves of a roof (fixed to the rafter feet) and to which the guttering is fixed.

Flashing
A sheet cut and fitted around joints in construction to weatherproof them.

Flitch beam
A site-formed beam comprising of two

timbers and a steel plate between, all
bolted together.

FCU
Fused connection unit in electrical
wiring used to protect part of the
circuit and enable safe maintenance.

Geotextile membrane
A permeable fabric that can be buried
without degrading to allow water
through but not soil particles allowing
free-drainage without clogging.

Hangars
Galvanised steel hangars for connecting
joists at right angles.

IC
Inspection chamber preformed in PVC-
U for rodding access on drains.

Joist
Horizontal structural timber making up
a floor or ceiling.

Lateral restraint
Fixing or designing to prevent
horizontal movement.

Levelling compound
A floor finish material of latex that is
self-levelling up to 6 mm thick.

Mesh reinforcement
Fabric steel mesh in sheets for
reinforcing concrete slabs.

MDPE
A strong resilient plastic used for
service (and some drainage) pipes.

Newel
The post at the top or bottom of a
staircase fixing the handrail.

Noggins
Cut pieces of timber packing between
joists or rafters to stop them twisting
(known as dwangs in Scotland).

Optimum start controls
Boiler controls that delay firing time
according to room temperature.

Oversite
The hardcore preparation beneath a
ground floor slab (also called sub-base).

PAR
Acronym for planed timber (prepared
all round).

Padstone
A hard bearing piece beneath a beam
designed to resist crushing.

Pitch
The angle of the roof or rafters.

Pressure system
A sealed heating and hot water system
with a pressure valve instead of a vent
in the header tank. See Combi boilers
and unvented cylinders.

Purlin
The horizontal structural timber in a
roof supporting the rafters often
halfway up.

PV (Photo-voltaic) tiles
Solar energy roof tiles that harness UV
light.

Radial circuit
A type of electrical circuit like a ring circuit but fed from one end only.

Rafter
The sloping structural timbers of a roof supporting the tile battens.

Racking
The name given to the movement of an element due to wind loads.

Ring circuit
Electrical circuit for power sockets that runs around part of the home joining up socket outlet and back to the distribution board.

RCD
Residual current device. Electrical contact breaker that monitors the earth wiring and switches the power off instantly if live current crosses to it. Pop-out switch acting as a fuse to prevent electrical overload.

Reed bed drainage
A natural means of cleaning foul water by filtration through reeds, the rhizomes of certain species are able to remove the bacteria and ammonia.

Render
External or internal base coat plaster.

Riser
The uprights between the step (tread) of a stair.

RSC
Square C-shaped steel beam (rolled steel channel).

RSJ
I-shaped steel beam (rolled steel joist).

Sarking
A roofing felt also used behind wall cladding for extra weather-resistance.

Screed
The level floor finish of cement and sand, between 50 and 75 mm thick applied to concrete floors.

Set
The finishing coat of plaster.

Shim
A wedge shaped packing piece for levelling windows, doors or wall plates.

Skim
The thin finishing coat of plaster applied over plasterboard.

Slipper
Drainage channel shaped as a bend for connecting drains inside a manhole.

Soaker
An undertile flashing to improve weather resistance.

Soffit
The board under-drawing the eaves of a roof beneath the rafter feet.

Specification
A written detailed description of work.

Solar gains
Internal heat generated by the sun through glazing.

String
The side board of a stair supporting the treads and balusters.

Supplementary bonding
Additional electrical earth bonding needed in bathrooms and WCs (identified as special location zones).

Swallet holes
Holes in the ground caused by water erosion.

Tread
The step part of a stair.

Trussed rafter
A factory manufactured roof member jointed with metal plates in a web of triangular shape. The members of each truss act holistically and not in isolation so they cannot be cut or altered without damaging the truss.

TRV
Thermostatic radiator valve fitted to radiator to switch off at a pre-set but adjustable temperature.

UB
Square I-shaped steel beam (universal beam) or column when used vertical.

Verge
The edge of a roof at the gable end.

Vertical restraint strapping
Fixing to prevent vertical movement (wind uplift).

Winder
A turning tread in the stair.

Wind Post
A structural post used where the buttressing masonry return is insufficient.

Y junction
A Y-shaped drainage piece for connecting one run to another.

Useful Contacts

**Approved Contractor Scheme
Institute of Plumbing**
64 Station Lane
Hornchurch
Essex
RM12 6NH
TEL: 01708 472791
www.plumbers.org.uk

**Association of Building Engineers
(ABE)**
Lutyens House
Billing Brook Road
Northampton
NN3 8NW
TEL: 0845 177 3411 or 01604 404121
FAX: 01604 784220
E-MAIL: building.engineers@abe.org.uk
www.abe.org.uk

**Association of Plumbing and
Heating Contractors**
14-15 Ensign House
Ensign Business Centre
Westwood Way
Coventry
CV4 8JA
TEL: 0800 542 6060
FAX: 02476 470942
EMAIL: enquiries@aphc.co.uk
www.licensedplumber.co.uk

**The Council for Registered Gas
Installers (CORGI)**
1 Elmwood
Chineham Business Park
Crockford Lane

Basingstoke
Hampshire
RG24 8WG
TEL: 01256 372200
EMAIL: enquiries@corgi-gas.com
www.corgi-gas.com

Electrical Contractors Association
34 Palace Court
London
W2 4HY
TEL: 020 7313 4800
www.eca.co.uk

FENSA Ltd
44-48 Borough High Street
LONDON SE1 1XB
TEL: 0870 780 2028
FAX: 020 7357 7458
EMAIL: enquiries@fensa.org.uk
www.fensa.org.uk

HETAS Ltd
PO Box 37
Bishop's Cleeve
Cheltenham
Gloucestershire
GL52 9TB
TEL: 01242 673257
FAX: 01242 673463
EMAIL: j.lake@blueyonder.co.uk
www.hetas.co.uk

Office of the Deputy Prime Minister (ODPM)
Planning Inspectorate
Tel: 0117 372 6372
Building Regulations
Tel: 020 7944 5746
www.odpm.gov.uk

Oil Firing Technical Association (OFTEC)
Foxwood House
Dobbs Lane
Kesgrave
Ipswich
IP5 2QQ
Tel: 0845 658 5080
Email: enquiries@oftec.org
www.oftec.org.uk

Royal Institute of Chartered Surveyors
Surveyor Court
Westwood Way
Coventry
CV4 8JE
Tel: 0870 333 1600
Email: contactrics@rics.org.uk
www.rics.org.uk

Timber Research and Development Council (TRADA)
Tel: 01494 569600
www.trada.co.uk

Acknowledgements

Thanks, as always, to my friends and colleagues. In particular:

Building Control: Liam, Martin, Paul, Steve and Trevor
Environmental Health: Penny
Planning: Maxine
Structural Engineering: Ratnam

Special thanks go to Carl, for combining his social visits with computer advice and leading a rescue operation, when the completed Chapter 7 simultaneously disappeared from my 'C' drive and backup disk.

Index